The Gentle Art
of
Wandering

The Gentle Art
of
Wandering

By David Ryan

New Mountain Books, Albuquerque, New Mexico

The Gentle Art of Wandering

First Edition 2012

10 9 8 7 6 5 4 3

Library of Congress Catalog Card Number: 2011962842

ISBN: 978-0-9776968-1-9

Also by David Ryan:

*Long Distance Hiking on the Appalachian Trail
for the Older Adventurer (2002/2012)*
The Bisbee Stairs (2014)

Photographs: David Ryan, except where noted

Book Design/Production: Carolyn Ryan Graphic Design

Typeface: Garamond, Optima, Didot

Published By:

New Mountain Books
2324 Rio Grande Boulevard NW
Albuquerque, New Mexico 87112 USA
612-889-964
www.newmountainbooks.com

All walks are good;
I don't know how long this walk is going to be,
But I do know one thing,
This is the best walk I have ever been on
Because this is the walk I am on right now.

- Lucky, an American Shepherd Hound

The Gentle Art
of
Wandering

Chapter 1

Several years ago, long before I met him, a man I know found a dinosaur while hiking in the backcountry of New Mexico. He and his partner were members of a committee that was responsible for identifying parcels of public land to consider for official wilderness protection. The area where they were hiking had already been taken off the list. They did not agree with the decision and had returned to the area to photograph prehistoric rock art in hopes of having the area relisted.

On the hike back to their car, they saw what "... *looked like a huge chicken neck laying half in and half out of the sandstone.*" In addition to the "huge chicken neck", they found a femur broken into three pieces lying on the ground. They were pretty certain that they had found part of a dinosaur, and when they showed pictures to a paleontologist, it was indeed confirmed as being a dinosaur.

The land in question was put back on the list and is now part of an official wilderness area, and the dinosaur, *Seismosaurus*, can be seen at the New Mexico Museum of Natural History in Albuquerque. It is the largest dinosaur ever found in New Mexico and one of the largest ever found anywhere. That "huge chicken neck" turned out to be part of the tail, and the total length of the dinosaur came out to be over 110 feet long.

The two hikers found *Seismosaurus* because they were wandering and exploring in the backcountry. And there is no reason why you can't find something amazing when you wander and explore. The idea behind *The Gentle Art of Wandering* is to

PHOTO COURTESY OF ONE OF THE HIKERS

This is what the huge chicken neck looked like in the ground! The ruler in the picture is 12 inches long. Can you imagine finding something like this the next time you go hiking?

help you develop the mindset to make every adventure on foot amazing.

Wandering is about cultivating the ability to use your entire body to "**see**" and experience all that is around you. *Seismosaurus* didn't erode out of the sandstone overnight. It was already there waiting for someone to see it. Who knows how many people walked by it without knowing what they had just passed. Maybe the angle of the sun was just right, but it might also be that two people came along who could **see** and who could recognize that this was something special and worth examining.

Adding the mindset of wandering to your outdoor activity puts you in position to find something unexpected and interesting when you get out. It could be as simple as meeting a new kitten on your walk home from work or it could be as dramatic as finding a dinosaur while hiking. Regardless of what you find, you will eventually discover that there is more for you to see and enjoy in this world around you right now than what the most

4   *Chapter 1*

This is how Seismosaurus looks today at the New Mexico Museum of Natural History.

imaginative fantasy writer could ever conceive. And I'll even go one step further; <u>you will always find something when you wander</u>. This is your opportunity to become your own Lewis and Clark.

But you will not find that dinosaur or become that Lewis and Clark if you do not get out. That's why it is important to briefly introduce the concepts of *idea, context, and action* before getting into the details of wandering. Everything we do involves all three of these components.

Essentially the combination of *idea, context, and action* is about giving you enough reason, background information and structure to get out. Some people need very little structure, while others need more. The important thing is for you to have enough ideas and structure to get out.

If we consider the two hikers who found *Seismosaurus*, they had the *idea* of photographing prehistoric rock art to provide evidence that the area in question deserved official wilderness protection. As for *context*, they knew something about the area, as they had visited the rock art before. This was enough for them to take motion. This was all the structure they needed to get out. It became the platform that allowed them to wander and find the dinosaur.

Fortunately most of us have plenty of ideas. But it doesn't hurt to keep your eyes and mind open to new ideas, as they can come from the most unexpected of places. Sometimes they can drop in your lap and beg you to act upon them.

I once had a conversation with a nursery owner[1] in Los Lunas, New Mexico who, after several years of searching, discovered a form of redwood or cypress tree growing in the wilds of New Mexico. Before his discovery, no trees of these species were known to grow in New Mexico except under cultivation.

The idea to search for the tree came to him when he was a student at New Mexico State University. He was told by the team leader in charge of restoring Socorro Mission, an old Spanish mission south of El Paso, Texas, that the timbers in the old church were a type of redwood. The present day church was built in 1843, but the roof beams (called vigas in the Southwest) were salvaged from the previous incarnation of the church built in the 18th century. As a Botany student, he knew that while Redwood species are found in many countries around the Pacific Rim, the only species found in North America were hundreds of miles away.

This was a mystery to him. Why would you travel that far when only 30 miles away in the Organ Mountains there is plenty of Ponderosa pine or Douglas fir to use?

When many of the Spanish mission churches were built in New Mexico and Texas, it was common practice for the labor-

---

1 Michael Martin Meléndrez; Trees That Please Nursery; Los Lunas, New Mexico; www.treesthatplease.us

These are the vigas that started the search for the trees. If you look closely, you can see that some of the vigas still have their original hand painted decoration.

ers to carry trees on their shoulders ten, twenty, and even thirty miles from where they were cut to the construction site. But shouldering a tree for hundreds of miles is completely out of the question. He believed that there had to be a closer source for the reddish wood, and he aimed to find it.

He spent his free time wandering through the streams and drainages that feed the Rio Grande north and south of El Paso. Several years later he was still looking. Finally, on one expedition, he revisited a watershed to see if he could penetrate it further. As he worked his way up, he noticed that a recent storm had scoured the channel. Everything looked new; it was as if he had never been there before. As he went further, he noticed for the first time an old tree stump. As he got closer he could tell that it was different than the other trees in the area. And when he got to the stump, he could tell that it was a variety of a cypress or redwood and that it could be the same type of wood found at the mission.

He continued up the watershed and checked every side channel. And then, there they were; two trees of a variety that he had never seen before in New Mexico. They were a form of a cypress or redwood and may be the trees he had been looking for. Even if the trees were not the exact same species as the vigas, they were still trees that had not been known to exist in New Mexico. He collected seeds and now grows them at his nursery.

The revealing of the tree stump is something that you'll want to remember for your wanderings. Change is constant. Every time it rains something is moved. Something old can be covered up, and something new can be brought to light. Even if you have been to a place several times before, it is still worth another look.

PHOTO COUTESY OF MICHAEL MELÉNDREZ
This is the tree stump that was revealed after a flood scoured the watershed.

Like the dinosaur, the trees and vigas with reddish wood were already there. But it took someone with the right mindset to notice that the vigas were made of a reddish wood that came from a tree no longer found near El Paso and then to develop the observation into the notion that there might be a remnant population of the trees hidden in some corner not too far away. In the case of the nursery owner, he knew trees, as he had studied Botany in college. For him the idea to search for the trees with reddish wood was dropped into his lap when he saw the vigas.

There is no reason why you can't use your knowledge to make a similar connection to develop your own wandering idea. The following chapters use real life examples to present many facets of wandering so you too can turn your own wandering idea into an amazing adventure of discovery.

PHOTO COUTESY OF MICHAEL MELÉNDREZ

These are the actual trees found further up the watershed.

Chapter 2

With your wandering idea in place, it's time to start wandering. As mentioned in the previous chapter, wandering is about **seeing** with your entire body. It is the ability to **see** that leads to discovering the unexpected. This is what will make any adventure amazing.

Along with general awareness, **seeing** involves three basic components: *common sense, recognition* and, for lack of a better word, *search image*. You already have common sense; it just needs to be tuned to what you are doing. Your basic <u>common sense</u> will help establish parameters to focus your wandering. This will improve your chances of finding something special.

The dinosaur finders from the previous chapter were not looking for a dinosaur, but they were walking through rocks that were deposited during the age of dinosaurs. So if the purpose of your wandering adventure is to look for dinosaur fossils, your common sense would have you go to an area where there are rocks from the age of dinosaurs. The nursery owner who found the trees with reddish wood was looking for the trees. In his case, his common sense placed him in watersheds where trees were likely to be.

Using your common sense, whether it is looking for archaeology sites in New Mexico or for an edible mushroom on the Appalachian Trail, applies to any activity. For example, if you are looking for an area where prehistoric people hunted, it makes sense to look downwind from a water source. If you are looking for a place where prehistoric people grew food and built their homes, common sense says to look where there is (or was) suitable moisture. If you happen to find an isolated artifact, common sense says to head uphill to see where it washed from. As you get more involved with your chosen activity, this will soon become automatic. It's just a matter of getting out there and getting some experience under your belt.

Recognition is having an idea of what something is when you find it. Certainly, if you are looking for edible mushrooms on the Appalachian Trail, you better know which ones are safe to eat. If you are looking for archaeology sites, knowing something about the artifact you just found will help you understand more about the area you are exploring. Recognition is a matter of knowledge, and knowledge is something that you can acquire over time. As your knowledge grows, you will be adding depth to your wandering experience.

I can use myself as an example of acquiring knowledge over time. When I moved to New Mexico, I hoped to get involved in archaeology. As much as I was interested in archaeology, I really did not know very much except from what I gathered during visits to National Parks. To add to my knowledge, I took classes, attended lectures, and joined up with a group of Bureau of Land Management (BLM) volunteers to look for archaeology sites on public land. I also learned to consult with experts and to ask questions when I ran into something that I was not sure about. I am by no means a professional archaeologist, but I am now proficient enough to go out on my own or with a partner to look for archaeology sites and to find amazing mysteries. And I still do rely upon experts to answer questions and keep attending lectures to learn more.

As important as common sense and recognition are to the **seeing** and discovery process, it is your search image capability that is the crux of **seeing**. This is setting aside the controlling portion of your mind (your ego) and letting your body's senses take over to **see**. It is something you feel rather than think. <u>It is letting something find you rather than your finding it.</u> As mentioned before, the two hikers who found the dinosaur were not expecting to find a dinosaur. It was just there and they were able to see it. This is something that cannot be taught or learned; it is something you just have to let happen.

To allow your body's senses to take over and let your search image capability kick in, it helps to be <u>present</u> and <u>connected</u> to the world immediately around you. This means quieting your mind so you can be right here, right now. If you are agitated and full of anger or replaying all that went wrong yesterday or anxious about tomorrow, you are not really here or present. You are somewhere else and will find it difficult to **see** what is right here, right now.

Our hectic lives and overwhelming responsibilities prevent many of us from being present and connected. If you are looking for a reason to wander, this may be it. You can let a wandering activity take you out of your normal routine and place you where you can quiet your mind and let yourself be right here, right now. When you do that, you can let yourself **see** and start discovering the amazing world around you. In this case, your wandering activity could be a form of walking meditation.

Turning down the noise of distractions and excessive outside stimulation will also help you become present and connected. It's pretty tough to connect with your immediate surroundings if you are checking your phone every few seconds for emails and text messages. It's also tough to spot something if you're bopping to music blasting through your headset. And finally it's hard to see what's on the ground if your eyes are glued to the electronic map on your GPS. It's hard to be connected to what's right here, right now if you are connected to a device.

I am not saying that you should not have electronic devices. I am, however, suggesting that you use them prudently and appropriately. You don't need to bring the office and its associated noise with you when you are wandering.

It will be easier for you to **see** if you can wander with beginner's mind. This means being open to everything and not letting your accumulated experience prevent you from seeing something new. This involves turning off your internal editor and just letting your senses accept information as it is provided. It's almost acting as if you have never been out before.

In the context of wandering, there is no conflict between using your common sense and recognition abilities and also going out with beginner's mind. As mentioned, common sense and recognition are about helping you discover and understand what you find. Beginner's mind is about being open to everything once you are out there.

In the beginner's mind there are many possibilities,
but in the expert's there are few.

Zen Master Shunryu Suzuki

Now that you are present and connected, let's see what you can discover. You don't need to walk in any special manner, but you certainly don't want to be a romper stomper hiker racing to the finish line. Normal walking is just fine.

Nor do you have to be as quiet as a Cistercian monk shuffling through a cloister to a predawn service. Normal conversation is fine, but you don't want it to take over and let it interfere with your awareness.

As for your eyes, let them relax and soften. The hardest way to find something is to go into "search mode" and overly focus your eyes. You might find the specific thing that you are searching for but you'll completely miss out on the unexpected.

This quieting is necessary because our active mind likes to be in control and wants things to be the way it wants them to be. The active mind finds comfort in patterns and will internally correct breaks in the pattern just to remain comfortable. That's why it is so easy for people to miss changes happening right in front of them, and why a policeman investigating a crime will get as many witnesses as possible to determine what happened. A policeman's expectation is that no one will have it completely right, but by piecing together little tidbits from here and there, he hopes he can reconstruct the story.

As you start to walk across the ground, you will notice that there are patterns. There is a way the vegetation is distributed and what vegetation is present. There is general slope and swale to the land. There is a way the land is being used. There is a texture and shine to the surface of the ground. There is a commonality to the look and placement of stones on the ground. All of these and more make up the patterns.

But by being present and connected, your senses can spot and bring to your attention something that is different and out of place. These are the breaks in the pattern, and noticing the breaks in the pattern is the essence of discovery. Rather than actively searching for something, let your senses and intuition reveal them to you. Much like when Sherlock Holmes solved a crime by noticing that the dog did not bark; that it did nothing.[1]

In a sense, your search image and recognition abilities will work together to make a discovery. While it is your search image capability that spots the break in the pattern, it is your recognition ability that interprets what that break might be. It's almost

---

1 *Silver Blaze;* **The Memoirs of Sherlock Holmes***;* Sir Arthur Conan Doyle

Enhancing Your Awareness

There are many techniques that you can use to hone or deepen your awareness. A good place to start is by listening. The next time you go on a walk or a hike consider stopping every now and then just to listen. You might hear an airplane flying overhead or a truck shifting gears in the distance. You might notice the birds around you and the different calls that they make. Or you might hear the quiet of absolute stillness.

As you continue your walk, you might notice how the sounds differ depending upon where you are. If you stop in a meadow, you might hear the buzz of bees moving from flower to flower. If you are deep in a pine forest you might hear the breeze whistling through the woods. In an aspen grove, the quaking leaves fluttering against each other might sound like the patter of a light rain. One of my most distinct memories while hiking on the Appalachian Trail was when thousands of grasshoppers were stirring the downed leaves, sounding as if they were making popcorn.

You can also emphasize other senses to deepen your awareness. You may notice how the light changes throughout the day. Or you could notice the shadows and how they get shorter and then longer as the day progresses. Or you might want to count how many different types of wildflowers there are in the next 100 yards.

Or you could notice the different smells as you walk through the woods. I still remember the distinct smell when walking through a forest in Pennsylvania full of thigh high ferns right after a rain. I wish I could assign a specific scent to it, but I can't. It was like breathing in peacefulness. The more you pay attention to these little things, the more automatic awareness will become. It will be what you do when you go out.

as if your senses (your search image capability) are telling your logical mind (recognition abilities) to, *"slow down, check this out; this may be way cool."* Because your recognition abilities do the interpretation, it helps to keep adding to your knowledge so you make better interpretations. But at the same time, you don't want your "expert" mind to discard what might be the find of the century.

As an example of search image capability in action, I can tell a story about when I was wandering in the backcountry of New Mexico and following a cow path through a deep arroyo. If you are not familiar with New Mexico, an arroyo is a stream bed that only carries water when it rains. Depending on the extent of erosion, an arroyo can be very deep and have very steep walls. The easiest way to cross an arroyo is to follow a cow path, as the cows have already figured out how to get to the other side.

I followed the cow path into the arroyo and then on to a shallow ledge at the bottom of the arroyo. The ledge was made of dried mud and was hard as brick. The ledge was punctured with four-inch-deep cow hoof prints. They too were dry and very hard. As I continued walking, a slight reflection from the bottom of one of the hoof prints caught my eye. I stopped to take a look. It looked like a piece of plastic that might have come from a jig saw puzzle. My immediate reaction was: what is a jig saw puzzle piece doing way out here? Then I thought it might be a piece from a board game like *Monopoly*, and again: why would something like that be way out here?

I bent over to take a closer look and then gently pried it from the dried mud. It wasn't a game piece or part of a jig saw puzzle. It wasn't even made out of plastic. It wasn't even something from this century. It was a small figurine or fetish of a ground animal made out of pottery from about 1000 years ago.

The fetish was only a couple of inches long and even had a little smiley face. It was amazing, and, when I came upon it, it had been lying upside down pushed into the bottom of a hoof print of dried mud on a ledge at the bottom of a very deep arroyo in the middle of nowhere.

There is no way I could have found the fetish, even if I was intentionally looking for it and spent the rest of my life comb-

Here's how I left the fetish in the ground. If you look closely at the fetish, you can see it's smiley face.

ing the area to find it. It found me! The reflection was the break in the pattern that my search image capability caught and then brought to my attention. If my search image capability had not noticed the break in the pattern, I would not have discovered the fetish. As mentioned previously, my initial reaction was that that the fetish was a piece of plastic. Fortunately, the curiosity of my beginner's mind led me to pry it out of the dried mud with my fingers to see what it actually was, and it turned out to be something incredible.

Another example of a search image capability in action is when a person[2] I know found what may be oldest example of Spanish rock art in New Mexico. In his case, he specializes in wandering in an area north and east of Albuquerque. He has also done considerable research on the area.

He was wandering along a dry arroyo that at one time was a major travel corridor. Today it is a seldom used dirt road. He had been to the area many times before and was following the corridor to see if he could find any inscriptions made in the rock by travelers from around 1900.

As he worked his way down the arroyo, he reached a sandstone outcrop with a flat wall facing the arroyo. He followed the wall. When the wall curved away from the arroyo, the sun cast an unusual shadow, and he caught a slight variation on the wall from the corner of his eye. He took a closer look and saw a cross carved into the rock.

The cross was about five feet above the ground and close to a foot and a half tall. He then noticed that there was another cross to the left of the first cross and then saw several smaller crosses carved at the base of the larger cross. As his eyes continued to relax and adjust to the light, he saw that the main cross was decorated with vines and had a halo at the top. To the side of the cross there was a very faint trace of a possible inscription.

He took several photographs and played with them on his computer when he got home. As he enhanced the photograph of the possible inscription, he saw what he believed to be letters with flourishes typical of 16th-Century Spain. As he worked with the photo more, he saw what he believed to be the name *Santa Maria*.

---

2 Mike Smith is a local historian whose specialty is the Sandia Mountains area of New Mexico. He is the author of many magazine articles and the book *Towns of the Sandia Mountains*.

He then went to the library to see if there was any significance to the name Santa Maria, and learned that there was a priest named Santa Maria who accompanied a small Spanish expedition into New Mexico in the 1580s. This would place the expedition after Coronado but before Juan de Onate established formal Spanish control in 1598. He also learned that the priest Santa Maria was last seen at a now long-gone village located, maybe at the most, a half mile away from the inscription. If there is a connection between the priest Santa Maria and the inscriptions, the inscriptions could be the oldest known Spanish rock art in New Mexico.

The jury is still out on the age of the inscription. Regardless of the outcome, this was an exciting find for my acquaintance, and clearly an example of one's seeing and discovering abilities in action. His common sense had him following the sandstone wall. His search image capability caught the variation in the wall. And his recognition abilities saw that it was rock art. He then added to his knowledge by taking pictures and learning about the priest Santa Maria. The combination of all of these made this a great wandering adventure.

■ ■ ■

As you become comfortable with relying upon your search image capability to spot breaks in the pattern, you will be amazed at how much there is to see all around you. You will find that you can't help but to see wherever you go. It will almost be like living in a whole new world. You will start noticing the variety of plant life, the abundance of little things that scoot along the ground, changes in sounds, the angle of shadows, and all that makes it wonderful to be outside on foot. And you will discover that you will always find something no matter where you are.

Test Your Search Image Capabilities

Can you see that one of the stones is a blade made out of chert (a form of flint) and how it differs from the other stones in the picture? It was carried into the area by prehistoric hunters. This area happens to be on the top of a ledge overlooking a spring. There were several other pieces of flint on the ledge. All of them were breaks in the pattern.

Can you see the small arrowhead made out of chert? It has a different texture and shine than the other stones. It too breaks the pattern.

The white spot near the center of the picture is a broken piece of pottery (potsherd). It too is a break in the pattern.

The discoveries that you make because of **seeing** are more than just objects. They are opportunities to connect and learn. When you come across an artifact such as the fetish found at the bottom of a hoof print or something like a piece of pottery feel free to pick it up. Regardless of what it is, hold it in your hand; hold it close to you; and examine it for its workmanship. On some pieces of pottery you can still see the finger prints of its maker.

As you do this, look around and think about what the maker's life must have been like. A thousand years ago, when and where the fetish was made, the only way people could get

Making Connections

(Top) What figure do you think the potter painted on the piece of pottery above? Can you imagine what the entire bowl looked like?
(Bottom) Is there a reason for the handprint, or was someone just having fun?

around was on foot. All of their tools were made out of stone, bone, or wood. Things that we take for granted such as a cold glass of water on a hot summer afternoon or a hot shower on a cold winter morning would have been beyond their comprehension.

When you examine something like the fetish, feel free to ask yourself some questions about it. What was it used for? Was it a religious object or a child's toy? Was it used once and tossed away, or was it cherished and kept for generations? And where did it come from? It certainly wasn't at the bottom of the arroyo for a thousand years.

Making Connections
(Top) Can you see the potter's thumbnail prints in piece of pottery above?
(Bottom) Is this the constellation Cassiopeia painted under this sandstone overhang? Can you imagine what the night sky must have been like when this star ceiling was painted several hundred years ago?

As you hold the object and ask these questions, you are giving yourself the opportunity to connect to something bigger than yourself and outside of yourself. Because of your discovery, you have made a connection and opened a window to seeing a whole different way of life. Making these connections may be what wandering is all about.

Once you have made your connection, leave the artifact where you found it. Leave it so the next person who comes along has the same opportunity as you did to make a connection. You don't want to collect the artifact and take it home with you.

There are many reasons for not collecting an artifact. Among them is that you could be breaking the law, and you are certainly taking something that is not yours. But the biggest reason for not collecting an artifact is that everything has a story, and if you take away something, you take away part of the story. In a sense, when you wander, you are wandering through stories. An artifact associated with the story belongs where the story is located.

There is always the chance that someone who can better understand the story than you will come along after you. If you have collected part of the story, that person may not be able to figure out the story or could come up with the wrong conclusions. Specifically, archaeologists in the Southwest use the combination of pottery types found on a site to date it. If you have collected one of the pottery types, an archaeologist could very easily come up with the wrong date.

As you wander you may want to consider the stories behind what you discover. Over time you may have learned enough to be able to combine what you find with your intuition to hear their stories. Being able to hear those stories will add depth to the connections you make while wandering.

The stories they tell

Everything you encounter while wandering has its story to tell. Although this book is not a manual on how to become an amateur archaeologist, I have used three different types of archaeology sites to illustrate how everything has its own story to tell. Telling these stories does not require that you to become a professional archaeologist. You can tell your own once you get a feel for what you are looking at. It will be a combination of what you have learned and your intuition. Your ability to do this will enhance your wandering experience.

This picture of a pile of stones is an archaeological site. An archaeological site can be the remains of a structure, a concentration of artifacts, or other evidence, such as rock art, of prior human occupation or use.

This particular pile, towards the rear of the picture, is a collapsed masonry room block that was used to store corn. The slight depression in front of the room block is a filled in pit house. This is where the people slept. The roof of the pit house would have been a plaza in front of the room block. This is where the daily chores were performed. Broken pottery in the vicinity of the site dates the site to around 1250 to 1300 CE.

This picture of broken pottery scattered on the ground is also a site. Instead of a structure made out of masonry, this structure was made out of adobe (dried mud). It eventually melted away. The fact that this site is in the open and that it melted away indicates that the people who lived here were at peace and felt safe.

Not everyone was so lucky.

This is what an adobe structure looks like after burning. The broken pieces of adobe have been baked into brick. If the fire gets hot enough, the adobe can turn into glass. Some of the pieces in this picture have been turned into glass as green as a Coca-Cola bottle. Sometimes you can even find the remains of corn cobs in the adobe pieces. The combination of burning and the site's remoteness indicates that there was warfare going on and that the people did not feel safe.

Chapter 3

With the basics of **seeing** and **connecting** under our belt, it is time to start looking into other aspects of wandering. If the basis of wandering is to make discoveries through **seeing**, an extension of this would be to let your discoveries guide you on where to go next. <u>Wandering is not a station-to-station journey; you have permission to change course.</u>

An example of this is when my archaeology wandering partner[1] and I visited a remote valley west of Albuquerque. We were asked by the Bureau of Land Management (BLM), where we are volunteers, to check on the condition of six known archaeological sites in the area. This is how we got the idea to visit the valley. For context we had the location of the valley and the GPS coordinates for the six known sites. We did not have high expectations for the valley as we had visited another area not too far away where we had found very little of archaeological interest. But we took action and drove on 35 miles of dirt roads to get the valley.

We found a place to park about one mile from the first known site and walked the rest of the way. When we reached the site location which was a spring, we did not find much of archaeological interest. A rancher had dug the spring out to make it easier for his cattle to get water, and anything of archaeological

---

1 When I go out looking for archaeology sites, I usually go out with my archaeology partner, Bob Julyan, and my dogs. When I refer to we, I am usually referring to Bob or my dogs. Bob is also the author of several books including **The Place Names of New Mexico** and **The Mountains of New Mexico**. His first novel **Sweeney** was recently released.

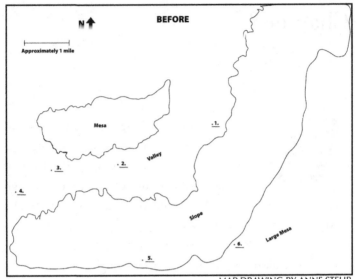

Before we visited the valley there were only six known archaeological sites.

interest was obliterated in the process. So far our low expectations for the valley were being met.

In all fairness to the rancher, many archaeology sites are very subtle and may only consist of a few scattered artifacts. If a site is subtle, traces of it can be easily washed away in a strong rain. So in all likelihood, it was not immediately obvious to the rancher that an archaeology site was being disturbed when the spring was reconfigured.

To continue with our examination of the sites, we headed across the valley by foot towards the second known site two and half miles away. The valley was very flat, but even a flat valley has a bit of a gentle slope. As we walked through the clumps of very short grass, we noticed that the grass was bent over in the direction of the water flow. <u>This is the type of a detail that only your search image capability would notice.</u> The bent grass was something that was different, and it broke the pattern.

As we continued walking we noticed an isolated potsherd tucked behind a tuft of grass on the upstream side. We didn't think too much of it at the time and figured that someone must have dropped a pot there many years ago. But then we saw another potsherd and then another. We then started seeing potsherds everywhere. At this point we decided to use our common sense and follow the potsherds uphill to see if we could find the source.

Because we were wandering and were not on a fixed station-to-station hike, we gave ourselves permission to change course. We were letting the potsherds choose our route and lead us to the source. And we did get to the source.

After running into to several pieces of pottery like this, we finally started uphill to find the source.

We found thousands of artifacts: broken pieces of pottery, flakes from stone tools, arrowheads, stones for grinding corn (manos and matates), hammer stones, and more. This was not one of the six known sites; this was a new site. After examining the new site, we then headed again towards the second known site, and found six more new sites before we reached it.

By the time we made it to the second known site, it was getting towards the end of the day and we knew we would need to come back to get to the rest of the six known sites. We have been back many times since that first visit. Even though it took us over a year, we finally made it to all six of the original sites. In the course of those visits we found over 100 new sites and discovered a prehistoric community that up until our visit no one knew existed.

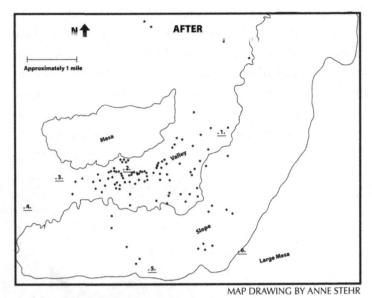

MAP DRAWING BY ANNE STEHR

Since we started visiting the valley, we have found over one hundred sites and counting! Each of the dots is a site location.

Had we been on a station-to-station hike with our search image capabilities turned off and with a limited goal of visiting the six known sites in the shortest period of time, we would have missed out on all of this. But we were not on a station-to-station hike; we were wandering. Wandering permitted us to change course so we could find the unexpected. But we would never have found the new sites if the BLM had not given us the idea to go out there in the first place and provided us the context of the six known sites. Our wandering abilities took it to the next level.

As for our original low expectations, they couldn't have been more off the mark and are another reason why it helps to go out with beginner's mind. Had we gone out with an expert's mind we could have missed all that this valley has to offer. Every time we think we're done with the valley, a new mystery pokes its head up to keep enticing us back. We may be coming back for a long long time.

Chapter 3

■ ■ ■

As you make wandering a regular practice, you will find that one wandering activity will give you an idea for a future wandering activity. In a sense, it is another variation of letting what you discover and **see** set the course of your wandering. It is a case of <u>one thing always leads to another.</u>

On the large mesa that borders the valley just described to the east, there is a low spot that would have held water in wetter times. Today it is a playa (a dried lake). The center of the playa has been dug out to provide a watering spot for cattle. The playa is bordered on three sides by a ridge.

Common sense would say that the downwind portion of the ridge would be a perfect place for hunters to prepare tools and observe animals. The ridge was begging us to explore it and we did.

We were not disappointed. My partner found what appeared to be part of a very old point. Experts later verified that it was part of a Folsom Point. Folsom Points date back to 10,000 years ago and were used for hunting bison.

The finding of that point is a good an example of how the combination of search image, recognition, and beginner's mind can work together to make discovery. Prior to finding the Folsom Point, my partner had gone out with a Paleo Indian expert several times. (Paleo Indians are prehistoric Indians from around the time of the last Ice Age, 10,000 years ago and before.) Because of those outings, he developed a deep interest in the stone tools of Paleo Indians. As we were walking the ridge, we were both **seeing** and recognizing pieces of flint on the ground. While I was content to keep walking, my partner's beginner's mind had him picking up each piece of flint to examine it closer, and voilà, he found part of a Folsom Point.

With a find this significant, we brought out a small group

of archaeologists and Paleo Indian specialists to the ridge. During that visit, we learned that the flint flakes on the ridge came from several different sources; some from as far as 300 miles away to the east in what is today Texas. The material for the Folsom Point happened to come from the Petrified Forest National Park area 150 miles to the west in Arizona. Other material came from closer sources. The variety of sources indicates that people walked a long way to track down animals to hunt, or that as far back as 10,000 years ago early hunters had established trading networks to exchange material.

The variety and distance of the flint sources gave us the idea of visiting one of the closer sources to see what it actually looks like. For context we had the name of the canyon where one of the sources is located, but we did not have the exact coordinates for the source. We studied the maps to determine how to get to the canyon and where to park. From there we had to treat looking for the flint source the same way as a prospector would look for gold. That is, you walk the canyon floor until you find the material you're looking for, and then follow the material through the canyon floor. When the material

MAP DRAWING BY ANNE STEHR

This map shows the source location for the flint we found on the ridge overlooking the playa. We decided to visit one of the closer locations sixty miles to the south.

ends, you then start heading uphill until you find the source.

We did exactly that, and we found the source. It was a mountain top of flint. Flint was everywhere. There were traces all over the mountain top of where hunters had knocked off pieces of flint to shape into weapons and tools. There was even a huge

This is what a flint source looks like. The entire mountain top was flint.

pile of discarded pieces of flint. It was an exciting little expedition that was a direct result of a previous activity; an example of one thing leading to another.

Continuing with the theme of one thing leading to another, when we were looking at the map to figure out how to get to the canyon just described, we saw that there was a spring only a few miles away. If we had time, we planned to check it out. It turned out that we did have the time, and we did check it out. While at the spring, we found several pieces of flint and an arrowhead on the downwind slope. We also found remains of buildings and other development in the immediate area.

The buildings and development piqued my curiosity, and when I got home I looked up the spring on the Internet. I learned that it is a warm spring, and that one hundred years ago, it had a spa. I also learned that there is a small little animal called a *Socorro isopod* that lives in that spring and only in that spring in the entire world.

This is the process of wandering. You find one thing, in this case a piece of flint at a Paleo Indian hunting site. And that generates the idea of looking for the source of the flint 60 miles away. With a limited amount of context, you find the flint source. And then, as a "by the way" while you're in the neighborhood, you check out a local spring that you saw on a map. And then you find something unexpected at the spring, the building remains, which then leads you to do some research on the spring. From your research you learn that the spring is a thermal spring and home to a tiny creature that lives in that spring, and only in that spring, and nowhere else in the entire world. And this leaves you with no other choice but to go back to the spring to see the little creature, and that is exactly what we did. And we did see the little guys swimming around in their bathwater temperature world.

For you, this process could become an unending cycle of one thing leading to another that could possibly last for the rest of your life. But that cycle cannot start nor be sustained without the ability to **see**.

■ ■ ■

People today are lucky to have so many new tools at their disposal to help them wander and to **see**. There are handheld GPS devices to record the locations of what you find. There is the Internet for conducting research. You can load electronic maps on your computer to plan your excursions and to document what you find. You can use a digital camera to record what you find at a fraction of the cost of processing film. And you can use Google Earth's aerial photography to look for places to wander and explore or to help answer questions.

When we were wandering a few miles north of where my partner found the Folsom Point, we ran into twisted bits of metal fragments. At first we thought that they were rusted buckets from an old ranch or mining operation. We later decided that they weren't. We then decided to look at the immediate area on Google Earth.

When we looked at Google Earth we found a series of concentric rings that looked like a bull's-eye target. A little more research confirmed that it was one of many bomb targets built during World War II to train Army Air Force bomber crews. With the additional context of the exact location coordinates provided by Google Earth, we went back out to see what the target looked like from the ground.

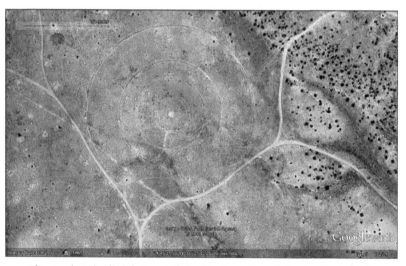

This is what the bomb target looks like from Google Earth. Notice the concentric rings.

The twisted pieces of metal were now obvious. You could easily make out the bomb casing, the tail fin, and the fuse mounted on the nose of the bomb to set off a small charge to mark where the bomb hit the ground. The target rings carved into the ground were harder to discern. If you didn't know that

(Above) This is what a bomb target ring looks like from the ground. If you didn't know better, you might think that it's an old road.

(Right) Here is a relatively intact bomb still laying on the ground.

it was part of the ring, you would think that it was the remains of a washed-out dirt road. This is something worth remembering; what you see in an aerial photograph is not necessarily what you can see from the ground.

Google Earth may not be very helpful if you are wandering in the woods. But if you are wandering in open country, it can come in handy for planning or for confirming where you have been. You may be able to use it to generate ideas for new adventures, and it could even come up with a few surprises.

As an example, for many years the State of Illinois has been acquiring land to develop a new airport far south of Chicago. To ensure that archaeological sites in the area were protected, a local amateur archaeologist who has since died took it upon herself to study aerial photographs of the area. She spotted what she thought might be a prehistoric Indian mound.[2]

There was definitely an elevated area that could be a mound, and there was a nearby depression that could be the "borrow pit". That is where the builders would have dug out the baskets-ful of dirt needed to build the mound. Several people were convinced that this was a prehistoric mound. Later investigations concluded that the mound was a glacial deposit.

Even though the mound turned out to be a glacial deposit rather than a prehistoric man-made mound, it was an exciting find, and a good example of what you can find through an aerial view. If you find something that catches your attention in Google Earth, remember that the aerial photograph is not enough. At this point it is only an idea with some context. You need to see what it looks like on the ground; this is when the real adventure and wandering starts.

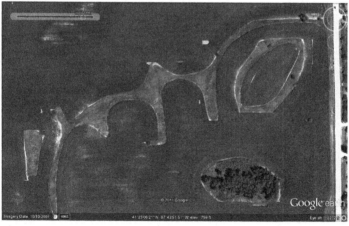

This is a Google Earth image of what some people thought might be an Indian Mound. The oval to the top right of the picture was thought to be the mound, and the wooded depression at the bottom of the picture was thought to be the borrow pit.

2 More information on this location is available at *http://www.dirtbrothers.org/Peotone/anomaly/anom.html*.

Chapter 4

The previous chapters used examples located in New Mexico or involved archaeology to illustrate the basic aspects of wandering. These are only examples; you don't have to be interested in archaeology or travel to New Mexico to wander. You can wander anywhere. The same wandering skills that work for discovering archaeology sites in the backcountry of New Mexico will work anywhere, even in a city as full of cars as Los Angeles.

Los Angeles may not be the first place you think of for an on-foot adventure. I know I used to think of freeways when I thought of Los Angeles, and I have my share of Los Angeles freeway horror stories to tell. If you've been there, you probably have your own freeway story to tell.

Los Angeles did not always have freeways. One hundred years ago people got around by trolley and the Pacific Electric interurban railway. More than anything else the Pacific Electric is responsible for the spread out nature of settlement in Southern California. Where the Pacific Electric went, houses were built, and the Pacific Electric went to every corner of the Los Angeles Basin. To make it easier for potential riders to reach the trolley and interurban lines, public staircases were built in the hilly parts of Los Angeles.

By the time the Dodgers moved to Los Angeles in 1958, this had all changed. By 1958 the city was firmly in love with automobile travel. Where there were once trolleys and the Pacific Electric to get you around, there were now freeways. Many of the freeways were built directly on top of the Pacific Electric routes. The handful of trolley and Pacific Electric lines remaining in 1958 were on their last legs and would be gone in a few short years. The public staircases, however, were still there and are still waiting for you to climb them.

I learned about the public staircases when I read a magazine article that described an annual stair walk organized by the author, Dan Koeppel.[1] Upon finishing the article, it seemed to me that climbing stairs as part of a trip to Los Angeles would be a perfect way to wander in a city and a good way to see how well the same techniques described in the previous chapters would work in an urban environment. It would also be a good way to see what additional aspects of wandering would be revealed by walking in an urban environment.

Dan Koeppel started climbing stairs several years ago to train for a mountain climbing trip. While looking for stairs to add to his training regimen, he learned that there was no official count on the number of staircases in the city nor a record of their exact location. He made it a personal goal to find as many staircases as possible.

He checked maps and city guides for streets with stub ends or with gaps in their route for potential staircase locations. He then visited the locations to see if his hunch was correct. Through his map work, general exploring and consultation with experts, he eventually found over 100 staircases. In the process of discovering staircases he had the opportunity to explore several neighborhoods that were new to him. To share his discoveries with others, he organized his annual walk which he calls The Big Parade. The walk covers 35 miles and 100 plus staircases in two

---

1 *The Big Parade*; **Backpacker Magazine**; September 2010 by Dan Koeppel; Dan also wrote an earlier article about the Los Angeles stairs; *I Climbed Los Angeles;* **Backpacker Magazine**; June 2004. If you are interested in learning more about the Big Parade, you can visit Dan's website, *www.thebigparadela. com.*

days. His technique for discovering stairs was not much different than the one I used for finding archaeological sites in the valley west of Albuquerque.

Dan Koeppel is not the only person looking for staircases in Los Angeles. Koeppel's associate, Bob Inman, has found over 260 staircases in the Los Angeles area and has published a guide to those stairs.[2] Another man, Charles Fleming, started climbing stairs in Los Angeles to see if that would cure his back pain and save him from going through another back surgery. He started with stairs near his home. As his back got better he moved on to other neighborhoods to find new staircases. His effort led to a healed back and a bestselling walking guide to the stairs.[3] His book has been the subject of many articles, blog postings, broadcast reports, and an upsurge in stair usage.

Stairs work for wandering because they were built for people traveling on foot. These are not ceremonial stairs in a large public space. These stairs are more functional as they are a short cut from a street at the top of hill to another street at the bottom of the hill. One hundred years later they still serve the foot traveler and provide a different way to explore a city and its neighborhoods. They are entryways to places that you may not normally visit. That was all I needed to hear to make the trip to Los Angeles.

I was chomping at the bit to go, but before I went I did some research on the stairs and the neighborhoods that I would visit. The research provided some additional context for the trip. I decided to make it a walking and wandering trip. Other than taking public transportation from and back to the airport, my time in Los Angeles would be on foot.

---

2 *A Guide to the Public Stairways of Los Angeles* by Bob Inman
3 *Secret Stairs: A Walking Guide to the Historic Staircases of Los Angeles* by Charles Fleming

Angels Flight and the adjoining staircase in downtown Los Angeles. This is where my Los Angeles wandering adventure began.

I chose Angels Flight, a small funicular railway in downtown Los Angeles, as the starting point of the trip for a number of reasons. The main one being that I could get there by public transportation from the airport.

My plan was quite simple, I would wander. Other than having a few items on my list to check out, I had no fixed route or set time table. I did buy a laminated *Thomas Guide* map of *Los Angeles and Hollywood Streets* to carry with me as a reference. My intention was to proceed in a northerly and westerly direction from Angels Flight until I reached the hilly neighborhoods of Echo Park and Silver Lake. They are a few miles northwest of downtown and a bit west of Dodger Stadium. Both neighborhoods have plenty of public staircases, and I expected to climb or descend staircases as I found them.

Very few of the staircases I found were noted on the map. So in most cases finding a staircase was a random event. The staircases determined where I went next. As stated at the beginning of Chapter 3, when you wander you have permission to change course and let what you find determine where you go next. Doing this turned out to be incredible. It was one of the most amazing trips of my life.

As planned, I started at Angels Flight, and rode the funicular car up and down. I then climbed the adjoining stairs to the top. At the top of the stairs there was a modern plaza paved with granite surrounded by tall buildings that didn't quite fit with the 1900s design of Angels Flight. I headed across the plaza, and within ten seconds something caught my eye. It was a large outdoor sculpture made of rust-colored steel beams. It looked like it might be a work by the sculptor Marc DiSuvero.

I know very little about art and am by no means an art aficionado. Looking for public sculptures in Los Angeles was nowhere close to being on my mind. The only reason that I had any inkling that it might be a DiSuvero sculpture is that my wife and I are very close friends with his sister, Marie Louise. It is through her that I have learned something about his style of work.

I stopped to look at the sculpture and walked around to see if I could find a nameplate. I finally spotted one on a distant wall and checked it out. It was a DiSuvero sculpture named *Pre-Natal Memories* and made out of Cor-ten steel. This was truly a serendipitous moment.

What are the chances of traveling to a city over eight hundred miles away from where you live, and then running into a sculpture that you didn't even know existed, in a plaza that you didn't know existed, that was made by the brother of a very close friend back home, ten seconds after reaching the top step of a public staircase adjacent to Angels Flight? If the word serendipity needs explanation, this is it. The same forces that allowed me

Pre-Natal Memories by Marc DiSuvero

My search image capabilities caught a glimpse of this sculpture and brought it to my attention.

to find the fetish in the valley west of Albuquerque came into play here.

I ran into the sculpture for three reasons. The first reason was that I was on a <u>walking trip</u>. Had I been on a driving trip to Los Angeles, and if Angels Flight was on my list of things to check out, I probably would have come nowhere near the plaza where the sculpture was located. I most likely would have parked my car nearby and then ridden Angels Flight up and down without getting off at the top. On the walk back to the car, I probably would have said to myself, *"... check that one off the list; next stop La Brea Tar Pits."* Getting out of the car and going on foot immediately increases your chances of running into pleasurable surprises!

The second reason that I ran into the sculpture was because I was <u>wandering</u>. I was not on a fixed route station-to-station expedition. I was not racing any clock. I was free to shift course and spend as much time or as little time as I cared on anything that caught my attention. If a sculpture such as this has nothing to say to you, you are not obligated to stop. You can keep moving. If it does mean something to you, feel free to stop. This is what wandering is all about.

The final reason that I ran into the sculpture was the combination of <u>search image and recognition</u>. My search image capabilities allowed me to catch a glimpse of the sculpture from the corner of my eye and brought it to my attention. I was able to recognize the style from what I had learned from the sculptor's sister. Had my search image capabilities been turned off, there is a good chance that I would have blasted by the sculpture without even knowing that it was there. But with my search image capabilities turned on, the sculpture said to me, "*...slow down, I might be interesting, you might want to take a closer look at me.*" <u>Interacting with your environment is the essence of letting something find you.</u>

After taking a couple of photographs of the sculpture, I continued on my way. One of the things that I had on my list to check out was an old subway tunnel built by the Pacific Electric in the 1920s. It has not been used as a subway since 1955. I had tried to see the tunnel on previous trips to Los Angeles but had missed it because I was always driving.

Trying to check something out in a different city while in a car is not easy. You're never certain about the neighborhood or where you can park or if the parking spot that you finally do find is close enough to what you want to see. And then there is the traffic. Will you finish up before rush hour? Can you make the turn, or turn around easily? And then there is the guy behind you blasting his horn because you're going 15 miles per hour while you are trying to figure out where you are. You finally get to the point of saying to yourself, *"… it must be over there somewhere"* and then drive on without actually seeing it.

The on-foot traveler has none of these issues. You have time to absorb and assess the nature of the neighborhood where you are walking to determine if it is the right place for you. In most cases it will be just fine. You don't have to worry about where to park. Nor how much it will cost or if it is close to where you want to be. And other than determining where to cross a street, traffic is not your problem. You have been liberated and are free to explore. And in my case, I was able to check out something that I had wanted to see for many years. Giving yourself the opportunity to explore and check out things too is part of wandering.

I did make it to the subway tunnel portal. It is now sealed and has a large mural of an old Pacific Electric car coming out of the tunnel. The old rail yard at the mouth of the tunnel is now a very nice apartment complex. Ironically, there was a public staircase directly above the tunnel for me to climb up and then back down.

As I walked past the apartment complex when I left the subway portal, my search image capabilities caught something of interest inside the apartment lobby. It was a collection of photographs and artifacts from when the area was an active rail yard; it was a small museum dedicated to what the area once was. I went into the lobby, and the doorman took me around to show me their collection. Again, if I was on a point-to-point journey, I would have blasted by the apartment building without noticing the display inside. Wandering allowed me to notice it and gave me the option of moving on or stopping to take a look. Wandering gives you options.

I then headed towards the hills. As I walked, I went through amazing neighborhoods with restored Victorian houses. I walked stairs as I found them, and even caught a glimpse of Dodger Stadium. To catch that glimpse, I found a path that took me behind a beautiful Ukrainian Orthodox church with redwood towers and gold domes. That path eventually took me to a hilltop neighborhood with views in all directions. I then worked my way to the Paul Landacre cabin.

I learned about Paul Landacre when I was researching neighborhoods before the trip. Landacre was a woodcut artist who lived in the neighborhood from the 1930s to the early 1960s. Many of his prints depict scenes from the neighborhood during his era. I liked his prints and added his cabin to my list of places to check out. His cabin on the side of a hill is now a City of Los Angeles historic landmark and is currently boarded up.

Learning, whether it is about a woodcut artist or something else, is an important part of wandering. You can learn while developing context for an adventure. You can learn as you wander. And then you can learn more afterwards when you research items you saw or discovered while wandering.

An example of seeing something and looking it up later was *Angelus Temple*. When I was walking by Echo Lake, I noticed a large building called *Angelus Temple* that looked like a combination of a church and an amphitheater. I didn't make a big deal about it at the time, but I did make a mental note to look it up when I got home. When I looked it up, I found out that it was the home base for Aimee Semple McPherson, the 1920s era celebrity and radio evangelist. Her name means very little to most of us today but her temple remains. A visit to the temple might be worth considering on a return trip to the neighborhood.

August Seventh by Paul Landacre 1936

Paul Landacre was born in 1893 and died in 1963. He lived in his Echo Park cabin from 1932 until his death in 1963. Paul Landacre made this drawing while living in the cabin. It depicts what he saw on a hot August day in 1936.

A street as steep as this is easier to walk up than down. If you look closely, you can see the famous Hollywood sign in the far distance.

The walk never ceased to be incredible. The neighborhoods were eclectic and diverse. Houses ranged from mail-order bungalows to architectural masterpieces. Many of the streets were so steep that that they were easier to walk up than down.

On some streets there would be a gap in the landscaping. In the middle of the gap would be a path leading from the street to a staircase. They were shortcuts to whole new world. On other streets you would come upon a large yellow diamond sign that said *END*. Beneath the yellow sign was a smaller orange diamond sign without words to reinforce that this was the end of the road. But if you looked behind the pair of signs, you could see that the road did not end for you and that you could continue wandering by climbing the staircase behind the signs.

Some staircases were relatively short, perhaps 50 steps, while others went on forever. Some had over 200 steps. Some stairs

The road may end for cars, but it doesn't end for those on foot.

were in great repair, while others were not. All were interesting. Some stairs had paths leading off to undeveloped tracts of
land and open space. Some stairs were the street and had houses
facing them. Others were like a trek through a jungle. On one
staircase I met a coyote. And on another I met a man with two
artificial legs. All the stairs led to new places to explore and kept
the wandering adventure moving.

One of the staircases led to a street that fronted a freeway.
The street eventually veered to left but the sidewalk continued
straight through a tunnel of shrubs. The shrub tunnel emptied
into a one-mile long remnant of the Pacific Electric. The right-
of-way has not been developed since the line shut down in 1955.
I learned about the remnant in my pre-trip research, and it too
was something that I wanted to check out. The right-of-way was
like a private open space for the neighborhood. The land is still

All of the staircases have their own special feature. This staircase has a path leading off to a hillside open space.

privately owned, but the neighbors[4] have been keeping watch over the area and have been working to get the land permanently protected as open-space.

The hills on both sides of the right-of-way made it seem like a canyon. There was even a staircase coming down from one of the hills to the right-of-way. At one time those stairs would have brought people down to a Pacific Electric stop. After about a mile, the right-of-way ended. The end was only a few hundred yards from the Los Angeles River. I strolled over to the river and saw herons and turtles. If one wanted, he or she could extend their walk by following bike routes and paths along the river for

---

4 One of the neighbors is Diane Edwardson. She calls the right-of-way the Red Car Property after the red cars of the Pacific Electric. She maintains a blog with information on the corridor and other items of interest in her immediate neighborhood, including public staircases and the Paul Landacre cabin, *http://redcarproperty.blogspot.com.*

The old Pacific Electric right-of-way provides a one mile long open space in the middle of Los Angeles.

several miles. But I was here to walk the stairs and turned around to find some more.

Wandering through Echo Park and Silver Lake was like a never-ending meal where each course of the meal got better and better. Every time I thought the meal was over, the waiter would bring out a new surprise that was even tastier than the one before. Even better about this meal, you never got full; there was always room for more. There were always new surprises, whether it was a cool building, a staircase, a patch of nature or something else. It was every bit as satisfying as walking along a beautiful mountain path. This too is part of wandering, finding something interesting everywhere you go. And to answer the question about if it is possible to wander in a city as filled with cars as Los Angeles. The answer is a resounding YES!

■ ■ ■

As you can see, public stairways are great for wandering and are an asset for any community that has them. Before leaving the topic of public stairways, I want to make a quick comparison between the Los Angeles stairs and the stairs 400 miles to the north in Berkeley, California. Where the new found popularity of the Los Angeles stairs has been the result of individuals' acting on their own, the rediscovery of the stairs and paths in Berkeley has been the result of a concerted public / private partnership.

When Berkeley started to grow after the San Francisco earthquake of 1906, land was set aside to build paths and stairways in the hilly parts of the community. The assumption was that the stairs and paths would be built to connect people to the trolley and interurban lines at the base of the hills when houses were eventually built. By the time actual building reached many areas of the community, people had stopped taking the trolley and were now driving cars. As a result many of the planned stairs and paths were never built. The land for the proposed paths remained idle and became overgrown.

When a major fire burned much of the hillside community in 1991, people discovered that they could not easily escape the fire and that firefighters could not reach parts of the fire because potential escape routes and pathways were overgrown. Because of this, the fire department asked the city to develop a plan to resurrect the defunct paths and stairways as a safety measure. The city contracted surveys and developed recommendations to clear and open critical paths. Like many communities, resources to implement the recommendation were not available.

In 1997 four women[5] got together and formed a group, *Berkeley Path Wanderers Association*, to do something about the paths. The Association's clear and simple mission statement was

---

5 Ruth Armstrong (Moskovitz), Jacque Ensign, Pat DeVito and Eleanor Gibson

and still is. *Dedicated to the preservation and restoration of public paths, steps and walkways in Berkeley for the use and enjoyment of all.* They worked with the city, raised money, organized scout groups and other people to get the job done. Their work has paid off. Today there are 136 paths, steps and walkways available for you to use. The Association even publishes a map of the paths to help you find them for your wanderings.[6]

---

6 The map can be purchased directly from the Association at *www. berkeleypaths.org.* Charles Fleming who wrote **Secret Stairs: A Walking Guide to the Historic Staircases of Los Angeles** has recently released **Secret Stairs East Bay: A Walking Guide to the Historic Staircases of Berkeley and Oakland**.

Other Stairs, Other Places

Los Angeles is not the only city with public staircases to support a wandering adventure. If you saw the 1973 movie **The Exorcist,** you know that there is a public staircase in the Georgetown neighborhood of Washington, D.C. Many other cities also have public staircases. If a town is built on hills or near a river, there is a good chance that you can find a public staircase. Pittsburgh, Pennsylvania is reported to have over 700 public staircases. (Pittsburgh also has two funicular railroads. Both of them are considerably larger than Angels Flight in Los Angeles.)

Incorporating a staircase or two from your neighborhood into a longer walk may be your opportunity to create a wandering adventure in your own community. Or, if you are traveling out of town, you may be able to create a little wandering adventure for yourself by finding a staircase and climbing it. Since climbing stairs in Los Angeles, I have enhanced my wandering adventures by climbing stairs in Portland, Oregon; Hood River, Oregon; Bisbee, Arizona; Cincinnati, Ohio; Amicalola Falls, Georgia; and New York City. (If you are interested in finding stairs to help in your wandering, you can consult a website maintained by Doug and Joan Beyerlein of Seattle, www.PublicStairs.com.)

To give you an idea of the diversity of the staircases and to highlight how they can help you wander, I'll briefly describe some those stairs.

The Hood River staircase had over 400 steps and crossed several streets on its route from downtown Hood River up the side of a hill to a residential neighborhood.

In Bisbee, an old Arizona mining town, the stairs wind throughout the old part of town. To honor and protect its staircases, the town hosts an annual 5K race in October called the Bisbee 1000. The race route includes several staircases and climbs over 1000 steps. They advertise it as the 5K that feels like a 10K.

Cincinnati is built on hills and, to no surprise, has many staircases. I spent a few hours on a Saturday morning wandering through the Mount Adams neighborhood and climbed several staircases while there.

On Good Friday in Cincinnati, thousands of people climb the stairs, some on their knees, to Holy Cross-Imaculata Church at the top of Mount Adams. When I walked that staircase, I met a woman who climbs the staircase on the first Saturday of every month to say the Rosary at every step. Perhaps, there is a similar opportunity for a Pilgrimage near where you live.

The southern terminus of the Appalachian Trail is on the summit of Springer Mountain in the far north of Georgia. There is no parking lot at the top of Springer Mountain. So if you want to start your hike on the Appalachian Trail at its terminus, you have to hike to the summit.

There are two basic choices. One is to drive on unpaved Forest Service roads to within a mile and half of the summit. The other choice is to hike the eight-plus-mile long Approach Trail from Amicalola Falls State Park in Georgia. If you start at the base of the falls, you have the opportunity to climb 604 stairs to reach the top of the falls. If you want to avoid the stairs and 800 feet of vertical elevation gain, you can start the Approach Trail from the top of the falls.

When I recently hiked a section of the Appalachian Trail, I chose the stairs. It definitely was a workout, especially with a backpack. But it was also a tremendous opportunity to get an up close look at the tallest waterfall east of the Mississippi River.

Tucked in a corner of New York City is the last remaining piece of the old Polo Grounds baseball park, the John T. Brush Stairway. It was built in 1913 to connect people living on top of Coogan's Bluff to the former ballpark below. Although the ballpark is long gone, the stairs are still used by local residents. The stairs are in poor repair today but they are scheduled to be rebuilt. All of the major sports teams that used to play in the Polo Grounds have contributed funds towards the rebuilding of the stairs. I was able to include the stairs while on a wandering adventure in New York.

If you are looking for the ultimate stair and wandering challenge, you can travel to Tai'an, China and climb over 6000 steps and gain 4500 feet in elevation to reach the top of Mount Taishan. It is the holiest of the five sacred Taoist peaks. It has been climbed by Chinese Emperors, Confucius, and Mao Zedong. My wife and I made the climb in 1996.

It is a walk like no other. Rather than a mountain path, it starts on the edge of the town of Tai'an as a broad flagstone paved staircase. Lining the staircase and off on little flagstone side paths are shrines, temples, and carved stone steles. You can spend hours wandering on these side paths and will find them all the way to the top. Along the way the stairs vary in width and steepness, pass through formal entry gates, and reach various guest houses and places to eat.

As we climbed the steps we passed porters with misshapen backs struggling with heavy loads hanging from carry sticks on their shoulders to deliver supplies to the various establishments at the top of the mountain. The loads could have gone up by cable car, but for some reason the porters went on foot.

We also met families dressed in their Sunday best, including smooth sole patent leather shoes, making the climb to the top of the mountain. Imagine walking up the side of a mountain with slippery shoes. Several families asked me to pose with them when they took pictures of the family in front of the various shrines. I was definitely the hit of the day.

And then we finally made it to the top, and it was only then that we realized that we just climbed a mountain. And it was on the trip down that we realized just how steep and narrow some of the stairs were. But we did make it down to join the countless thousands who have also had this incredible wandering experience.

Chapter 5

The previous chapter made several brief mentions of old right-of-ways, path routes, undeveloped parcels of land, natural areas and open space within the context of wandering through Los Angeles. All of these are examples of a **Corridor** or a **Crease**. When urban development came, the natural world did not disappear. It retreated to the corridors and creases.

Corridors are linear in nature and are found along abandoned rail right-of-ways, levees, utility easements, and abandoned roads. **Creases**, on the other hand, are tracts of land that are usually too difficult to develop, or are inaccessible to development. They are oftentimes along the edges, hidden behind something else, in land cut off by a railroad, along a watercourse, or in the case of Los Angeles along steep hillsides. Nature thrives in all of these. They are perfect for wandering.

Creases and Corridors can be found almost anywhere. The Calumet Region in southeastern Chicago and northwestern Indiana at the foot of Lake Michigan is one of the most heavily industrialized places in the world. It is named after the Calumet River which begins and ends in the area. At one time the Calumet Region was the nation's leading producer of steel. In the middle of the last century before environmental safeguards were put into place, a permanent red cloud loomed over the area and coated almost everything with red soot.

The red cloud and many of the steel mills are now gone. Despite the closings, many mills still remain. The combination of mills, power plants, oil refineries, and the maze of railroad tracks, busy roads, tank farms, and fences still gives the area a heavy industrial feel.

Prior to the steel mills, the land was a maze of sand dunes and wetlands that was thought to be unsuitable for development. Many of the sand dunes were close to 200 feet tall. Before European settlement, the area was a favored hunting ground of the Potawatomi and Miami Indians. With the arrival of Europeans, this became prime trapping grounds. According to a history of the area published in 1915[1], more than 10,000 muskrats were trapped every year in the mid-19th century.

Later in the 19th century, "Gilded Age" sportsmen clubs moved into the area. Their purpose was not to hunt or trap animals for sustenance; their purpose was to provide a luxurious, comfortable, and convenient platform for shooting wild animals. The Tolleston Gun Club controlled much of land where Gary, Indiana now stands today; its roster was a who's who of wealthy Chicago industrialists. If the accounts can be believed, it was Armageddon for animals: one small group of hunters shot 1200 birds in two days; one person set the club record by shooting 189 birds in less than four hours (that's almost one a minute); and one trapper took 3000 muskrats in one year. There are no overall statistics available, but the totals must have been staggering.

The region's proximity to Chicago, access to Lake Michigan, and location on the nation's major east-west rail lines led to heavy industrial development by the end of the 19th Century. The Gary Steel Works, U.S. Steel's largest mill, opened in 1906. The location was perfect for making steel. Railroads brought in coal from southern Illinois and Pennsylvania. Ore boats brought

1 Howat, William Frederick M.D.; *A Standard History of Lake County, Indiana and the Calumet Region*; 1915; The Lewis Publishing Company, Chicago and New York

in iron ore from the Lake Superior region to a harbor carved out of the dunes at the southern end of Lake Michigan. And the railroads delivered the finished product across the nation.

In the process of development, dunes were leveled and wetlands were filled or drained. Fortunately a good portion of the landscape was saved by the creation of the Indiana Dunes State Park and the Indiana Dunes National Lakeshore. The checkerboard nature of development and the crisscross of railroad tracks left many isolated pockets of dunes and wetlands throughout the area.

The decline of heavy industry has made it possible for the railroads to consolidate their operations and abandon unneeded lines. These former rail lines provide perfect corridors to penetrate the area to discover creases where nature still rules. And along an abandoned rail corridor of the Indiana Harbor Belt Railroad nature does rule.

The abandoned rail corridor begins only a few hundred yards from a looming steel mill and a huge pile of slag. It ends a few miles later at another steel mill. Along the way the corridor passes by a few residential areas but most of the land is wild with tall sand dunes covered with oaks and maples. Between the dunes are ponds, marshes and bogs. Part of the area is an oak savannah where the oak trees are spaced far enough apart for tall grasses to grow between them. A third of mile south of the corridor there is a live rail line. The area sandwiched between the two is an untouched crease.

When I walked the corridor with my sister, we saw white tail deer, muskrat and beaver lodges, a beaver swimming across a pond, herons and other wading birds feeding, incredible moths, beetles, tiny lizards, dozens of turtles, ducks, and fish. The variety of vegetation was amazing. There were oaks, maples, ferns, shrubs, and abundant wildflowers. We even saw prickly pear and

A typical scene of the crease from the corridor. It would have been very difficult to get this close to lands this wet without the corridor.

crypto-biotic soil in a blow-out in one of the sand dunes. You would expect to find this in the semi-arid Southwest. But it was a complete surprise to find them in the moist Midwest.

The diversity of area was recognized by biologist Henry Cowles over a century ago. And it was here in the dunes area that his studies on plant succession and the interactions of different life forms made him one of the founding fathers of ecology.[2]

Even though this particular corridor borders a heavily populated metropolis and starts within spitting distance of a huge steel mill, it was quiet and peaceful. The only noise was from the haunting horn of a passing freight train running on the live rail line to the south. Without the abandoned rail line to use as a corridor, it would have been very hard to work your way through the wet soil and undergrowth to penetrate this crease.

---

2 To learn more about Henry Cowles and the biology of the Calumet Region, please see page 10 of *The Indiana Dunes Story: How Nature and People Made a Park*, 1984, Shirley Heinze Environmental Fund

The combination of a corridor, crease, and the ability to **see** can make even the most simple of walks amazing. There is so much going on everywhere. All you have to do is to get out there and let yourself see it. Corridors are an invitation to you to enter and wander.

■ ■ ■

Corridors can also be used as a link in an overall route or as a connector to another route. There are old corridors everywhere. According to the *Rails-to-Trails Conservancy*, railroad track mileage in the nation peaked in 1916 at over 270,000 miles. Since then, over 150,000 miles have been abandoned and almost 20,000 of those miles have been put back to use as rail trails. When you add in the other candidates such as river banks, utility corridors, abandoned trolley lines, and many others, the opportunity to find a corridor for wandering is virtually unlimited.

I found the Calumet Region corridor and many others like it when I was scouting out a bike route between Chicago and Washington, D.C. When I eventually made that trip, I was able to stay off roads for over half of the distance by riding on rail trails, rail corridors that were not rail trails, canal towpaths, ditch banks, utility corridors, and even user-created trails. In one case, I followed a user-created trail at the end of the official rail trail through a hole in a fence to a trail on a ditch bank. That same route could also be used to support a long distance hike or a great day of walking and wandering.

A couple of years ago I read in the newspaper[3] about a woman from Montana who is riding around the country on horseback. She travels with two horses (one for her and the other for her gear) and her dog, and on the date of the article she had

---

3 *Lone Rider*, **Albuquerque Journal**, December 10, 2009 by Rosalie Rayburn; the article is about Bernice Ende and her ride on horseback across the country. You can follow her progress on her website, *www.endeofthetrail.com*.

Map Example (1)

USGS (United States Geological Survey) topo maps are good places to look for corridors and other geographic features. This particular portion of a topo map from New Mexico shows an old railroad grade, pipeline, power line, and a cluster of springs.

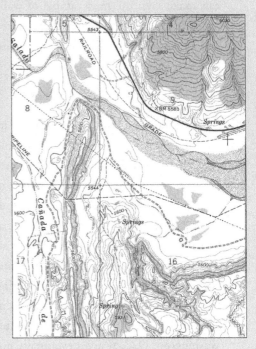

The cluster of springs in the lower center of the map is actually the most interesting feature in the area. They happen to be mineral laden warm springs that have built large travertine domes as shown in the picture below.

Map Example (2)

This topo map portion is from the Calumet region in Indiana. The dashed line crossing the map at an upward angle is an old rail corridor. This is one of several corridors in the area and is not the one described in the text. The bridge over the river shown in the map is still intact. When I hiked through the area it was a maze of meadows, wildflowers, wetlands, and small dunes.

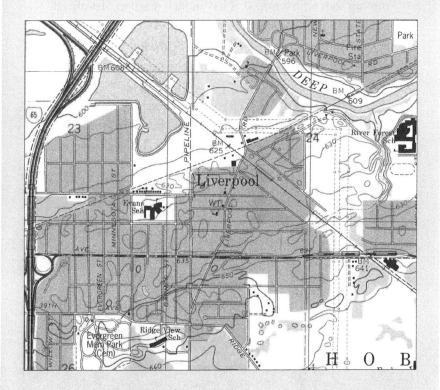

ridden over 13,000 miles. She uses maps to identify corridors that will get her to her intended destination. She follows dirt roads, railroad lines, power line corridors, canals, and anything else that will help her cross a river, keep her away from traffic, and to make her trip safe.

If you are interested in finding a corridor where you live, you can start with a map that has enough detail to identify rail, utility, and ditch corridors (see pages 66 and 67). That same map might even identify an abandoned rail corridor. Once you find something promising, you'll then have to get out and see what's actually there.

Another option is to keep your eyes open for potential corridors when you drive around. A good way to spot a corridor is to check out an overpass when you drive on it. If there isn't a road

This is a typical path you can find along a corridor.

or railroad track underneath, it is most likely a rail corridor that was abandoned after the overpass was built. The same would apply when you go over rivers and utility corridors. Check to see if there is a ditch bank or lightly used service road that could be used as a corridor. As you drive, keep an eye out for old rail roadbeds along the road or veering off at an angle. They too may be a good corridor.

When you do find a corridor, keep in mind that the ownership of the corridor may be unclear. In some cases the railroad may have only had an easement to cross someone's property. In that case, there is a chance that the ownership of the corridor reverted back upon abandonment. In other cases the corridor may have been acquired by a local government or organization to save for use as a future trail. Sometimes an old corridor may be acquired by an adjacent utility or industrial concern to provide a service road to access their property. In other cases the land may be privately owned and in limbo until it is developed. As long as there is no fence blocking access or a *No Trespassing* sign, I would consider checking it out.

■ ■ ■

Corridors can sometimes be found in the most unlikely of places. In Portland, Oregon there are several thousand acres of naturally forested land and many miles of hiking trails right in the city. This is an obvious hiking and wandering resource. Portland also has another and very unlikely wandering resource, its many miles of unpaved streets. You can combine various sections of unpaved streets to make a corridor linking you to a series of creases. Since the city has no plans to pave these streets, they should be available for you to use many more years or, perhaps, forever.

Some of them have been repaired by neighbors and are usable by cars. Some of them are cratered and require a jeep to get through. Others have been taken over by neighbors to use as gardens. Some have been reduced to one lane and others to only a footpath. All are available to the wanderer to develop an interesting walk.

One day my grandson and I started walking on the unpaved street in front of his house. Through a combination of unpaved and paved streets, we reached a parcel of land that the city park district has recently bought to set aside as a natural area. Other than having a couple of paths, the natural area remains undeveloped.

We followed one of the paths into the natural area. When we reached a pond in the middle of the woods, we saw an old abandoned building deeper in the woods. We looked around and found a little-used side path to get a closer look. We were able to reach the building, and it was creepy. It felt like it was haunted. Hanging on the gate was an even creepier poem about life and death. Sufficiently freaked out, we followed another path out of the woods and found our way to an old trolley line that is now a paved bike path. The bike path corridor also has a nearby hiking path following a creek.

We took the hiking path along the creek. As we walked we saw turtles and other wildlife and passed through huge raspberry patches. One could make a feast during berry season. When it was time to head home, we noticed a path heading away from the creek and took it. The path soon reached an unpaved street. The unpaved street varied on every block. In some places the unpaved street disappeared and became a path. Eventually the unpaved street came to an end and we had to take a short path through a tunnel of shrubs to land on the same street where my grandson lives to complete the loop. In a few minutes we were home.

The unpaved streets of Portland do not warrant a special trip on your part to check them out. They are, however, an example of how you can use an unlikely resource right in front of your nose to create an interesting walk and to give you an opportunity to make unexpected discoveries.

In Chapter 3 the idea of letting what you **see** guide you in your wandering was discussed. <u>In the case of the unpaved streets, it is letting your creativity and curiosity guide you in your wandering.</u> The creativity comes into play by looking at that unpaved street as an asset rather than as an eyesore. The curiosity comes in asking yourself where does this path, road, route, or whatever go, and then taking action to wander along it until you find out. Or asking yourself, how do I get over there (as in the case of the creepy building with the creepy poem sitting in the middle of the woods) and then finding a way to get there. Asking and acting upon your questions helps you run into surprises and to make discoveries.

Is there an unpaved street, or equally unlikely place, near where you live that you could incorporate into a wandering adventure? I know where I live in New Mexico that there is a network of small irrigation ditches (*acequias* in Spanish) in the Rio Grande valley. The acequias have been there for hundreds of years, and one could follow them for days for a wandering adventure.

Continuing with the idea of looking at something differently and turning it into an asset, you may want to consider another example from Portland. A few years ago, the Oregon Health and Science University (OHSU) invested a large sum of money to build an aerial tram to connect its main hilltop campus to a new satellite campus down below on the riverfront. While it was still under construction, Don Baack, who chairs a community committee[4] that promotes walking and biking trails in the southwest section of Portland, Oregon, and his son Eric were discussing if anything could be done to make the aerial tram a public asset to help justify its cost. Eric came up with the idea of using existing hiking trails to connect the aerial tram to other modes of transit in Portland. This was the kernel that became the *4T Trail.*

As they hashed it out, the *4T Trail* would be a loop route with four distinct links: Trail, Tram, Trolley and Train; hence the name 4T. The Trail portion would begin near the Portland Zoo and use existing hiking trails to go over Portland's highest point at Council Crest and then eventually reach the OHSU hilltop campus. The Tram portion would descend from the hilltop to the riverfront where there is a trolley stop. The Trolley portion would be the Portland Streetcar. The Streetcar connects new development north and south of downtown Portland to the center city. The trolley would be the link to downtown for connecting to the MAX Train. MAX is Portland's light rail network and would be the Train portion of the trail to take you back to the zoo to complete the loop.

With the concept in place, Don and his committee put in the hard work of making the 4T a public reality rather than a private fancy. They did the necessary planning to determine what

---

4 Southwest Trails, www.swtrails.org

the trail should be and established a budget for what it would cost ($45,000). They pitched their plan to the City Council and got a great reception but no money. The Mayor, however, took an interest and gave them the money they needed to make the 4T a reality from his discretionary funds. Don and his committee took it from there. They hired an artist to design a logo and develop a theme for signage and collateral material; they finalized a route; and they had signs made and erected. And voilà, the

4T Trail was completed within budget and opened for business.

I had the opportunity to do the 4T with my wife, daughter, and grandson and it was a blast. We began our trek at the Portland Zoo and followed the 4T signs for a couple of blocks to one of Portland's naturally forested areas. There the trail entered the woods and followed a water course up a deep ravine on the side of a mountain.

There was some highway noise when we entered the forest. But it soon disappeared and became quiet. With Douglas fir and cedars above us and bright green ferns and ivy below it was a deep forest in the heart of the city. The quiet allowed us to notice the little things around us: the different kinds of fungi; the thick moss; the slick tracks of snails and slugs on the trail; the burrow holes of small animals; new cedars growing out of old stumps; and the remains of now abandoned developments. In some places there were houses hanging over the edge of the ravine. Their only support seemed to be very thin poles. We even spotted a full-size totem pole in someone's yard.

We eventually reached the top of the trail at Council Crest. There we saw signs describing how it once had an amusement park served by a trolley line. Near the top of the crest was a marker stone that described a former stop for the trolley line. To the right and left of the marker you can still see remains of the old trolley right-of-way. From the top of the crest we followed the trail down the other side of the mountain, and when we reached the bottom we took another trail up to OHSU. There we caught the tram, trolley and train combination to return to the zoo. It was a perfect combination of walking and transit to make for a great afternoon of wandering. The hiking portion of the trek was a comfortable four and half miles that included about 800 feet of elevation gain.

The *4T Trail* and the *Berkeley Paths*, mentioned in the previous chapter, demonstrate what a few energetic people can accomplish to make a great addition to their community. They both are examples of looking at something already in place in a different way to create an entirely new asset for their community. Is there something similar you could be looking at differently to create a resource for your community?

■ ■ ■

In addition to finding creases along corridors, you can also find them in land in transition or isolated from development. In 1912 John D. Rockefeller's daughter built a lavish country estate on 300 acres overlooking Lake Michigan sixty miles northwest of the Calumet Region in the northern suburbs of Chicago. Rather than the dunes and wetlands of the Calumet Region, the dominant feature of this area is a moraine deposited along the lake front during the last Ice Age. Because of the moraine, the lake shore in this area has a very steep bluff with several very deep ravines cut into the bluff. The combination of bluff and ravines creates a landscape unlike the rest of the Chicago area. The interior of the ravines even has a different micro climate and ecosystem than the top of the moraine.

After John D. Rockefeller's daughter died in 1932, the buildings of the estate fell into disrepair and the grounds and formal gardens became overgrown. Twenty plus years later the property was sold for back taxes. The main house was beyond salvage and the new owners had to tear it down. While the new owners were deciding what to do with the land, the overgrown estate grounds became a favorite place for many to explore. When the land was finally redeveloped for housing in the 1960s, a portion of the land wedged between a ravine and a military facility was left undeveloped. The local community was able to acquire the undeveloped land to keep it as a nature preserve.

And like the rail corridor in Indiana, nature rules in this crease. The best thing about this protected parcel is that it is unpublicized. There are no signs announcing its presence; there is no nearby parking; and if you want to visit it, you have to park far away and hope you can find it when you walk in. But if you can find it, you will be well rewarded with a secluded trail through a quiet hardwood forest that eventually follows a ravine down to a secluded beach along Lake Michigan.

When I visited this crease with my sister on a very nice Saturday morning, we had the trail to ourselves. There were plenty of people out riding bikes and running errands nearby, but the crease was ours alone. That is except for the red fox that we saw as we entered the trail, several white tail deer, squirrels, and other animals that scurried away from us. The beach too, except for the seagulls, was empty. There were no sunbathers, no swimmers, and nobody having a picnic. There was just quiet except for squawks from the gulls and the gentle lapping of the waves. Finding a quiet place to spend a Saturday morning in a populous metropolitan area is not a bad result of a short hike.

Taking a time out from the world of noise, manufactured drama, and overstimulation is a good reason to get out and wander. When you find a place that is quiet, you can let the world around you just happen. You can start the process by getting out of the car and shifting yourself to a world that only moves at the pace of your step. If you can let yourself be present at this very moment, you will discover that there is already plenty going on around you and that any additional noise or stimulation will only drown it out. You will see that a small patch of ground is full of life and that you could spend hours discovering all that it has to offer. And if you just listen, you can hear how the sound varies as the day moves on. As you spend more time in quiet places you will see how everything, including yourself, is part of the moment and how lucky we are to be here.

■ ■ ■

It may not be a major stretch to find a crease in a suburban area or in a smaller city such as Portland, or even in a city as spread out and hilly as Los Angeles, but is it possible to find a crease on the island of Manhattan? Certainly walking is a way of life in New York[5] and you could spend your entire life wander-

---

5 Legendary tennis great Billie Jean King, who is on the *President's Council on Fitness, Sports and Nutrition,* made the comment on a television news show (*Morning Joe,* MSNBC, June 15, 2011) that New Yorkers live 2 ½ years longer than the national average because they walk everywhere they go.
I checked the Internet to see if this was true. I couldn't find the exact number of 2 ½ years, but I did learn that New Yorkers do have longer life spans. I am sure many factors go into life expectancy, but I would guess that walking everywhere has to make some contribution. I doubt if anyone would claim that New York City is a laid-back, low cost, stress-free place to live. So something positive must be in the mix somewhere for New Yorkers.

Chapter 5

ing the streets making new discoveries every day. But is there anything that would resemble a crease?

Over a half a century ago, Cy Adler[6], founder of *Shorewalkers* and a life-long New Yorker, set out to find quiet places to walk by staying as close to the edge of Manhattan along the waterfront as possible. Over time he expanded his walks to include all of the city's boroughs, and has even traced a route fifty miles north along the Hudson to Bear Mountain. He tries to get as close to the water as possible but he obviously has to accommodate obstructions by making detours away from the water. By doing this he has discovered many obscure corners and creases within a huge city. He has also seen a remarkable amount of change since he started his walks.

What he has seen has been revolutionary. When he started walking, the shore of Manhattan was industrialized. It was the major port of the country. There were piers one after another at the end of almost every street on the southern half of Manhattan along the Hudson. There were railroad tracks along the shore and trains shuttling freight in and out of the piers night and day. The harbor waters and Hudson River were alive with ships, tug boats, and barges. There were even barges built to move railroad cars from one side of the Hudson to the other. It was a swirl of activity and movement. And there were the longshoremen who looked like they stepped off the movie set of *On the Waterfront* loading and unloading ships one crate at a time.

---

6 In addition founding Shorewalkers, Cy Adler has published two guide books on walking along the shore: *Walking Manhattan's Rim: The Great Saunter* (2003) and *Walking the Hudson, Batt to Bear: From the Battery to Bear Mountain* (1997). Both books are published by Green Eagle Press, New York. More information is available at www.shorewalkers.com.

The container[7] has changed all of this and has revolutionized how we live. There are no longer cargo ships docking on the shore of Manhattan; the container facilities are all down river in New Jersey. Longshoremen are no longer needed to unload cargo by hand; today cranes lift the containers from the ship and drop them right on the truck or railcar making the final delivery. Where it used to take days to unload a ship, it now only takes a few hours. Today, once a carton of merchandise leaves its point of origin, it is not touched until it reaches its final destination. This has eliminated the extra time, cost, and shrinkage of loading and unloading cargo every time it is transferred to a different mode of transport. The impact has been huge. The longshoremen are gone and the waterfront has become a place for recreation and living rather than a place for industry.

But the impact of the container goes beyond the shore of Manhattan; it is has changed how we live. With the huge reduction in transportation costs, low-priced goods from overseas can easily compete with products made across the street. The result is that instead of watching a television set manufactured in Chicago, we now turn on a set made overseas. Even if the set were assembled across the border in Mexico, many of its parts would have been made overseas and shipped to the assembly point by container. The container has not only affected consumer electronics; it has touched almost everything that we buy. And Cy Adler saw this revolution happen right before his eyes as he walked and explored the shores of Manhattan.

As you wander, you may want to think about the changes that have occurred where you are walking. I know that, where I wander in the New Mexico backcountry, I have found evidence

---

7 If you are interested in learning more about the container, **The New Yorker** ran a brief but very good article, *The Financial Page: The Box that Launched a Thousand Ships,* by James Surowiecki on page 46 of the December 11, 2000 issue.

Chapter 5

of every phase of human occupation starting from today and going all the way back to 10,000 years ago. Something similar may be waiting for you where you wander.

Cy Adler's organization, *Shorewalkers*, sponsors several walks each year to encourage people to explore the edge of New York. Their biggest walk of the year is *The Great Saunter*. It saunters around the entire 32 mile circumference of Manhattan in one day. I decided to go on a *Great Saunter* just to get the feel of what it would be like to walk on the edge of Manhattan.

It was a great way to see New York and an opportunity to go through neighborhoods that I wouldn't normally have thought of visiting. It was amazing to see how the piers along the Hudson have been removed or transformed into parks, tennis courts, and baseball diamonds. From the walk route you can even catch a glimpse of *The Highline*, a former rail structure that is now being converted into a landscaped pedestrian park. In fact, most of Manhattan is now surrounded by a green belt of parks, bike

Pier 49 today

paths, and a walking promenade. So that the past is not completely forgotten, the former pier locations are noted with granite markers with their pier number carved into them.

As the walk approached the northern tip of Manhattan, it went through a heavily wooded park with rugged terrain. When the walk swung around to the east side of Manhattan it went through several diverse and lively neighborhoods until it reached another promenade along the Harlem River. When the walk reached the location of the old Polo Grounds, the former home of the New York Giants baseball team before they moved to San Francisco, I couldn't resist the temptation to take a short de-

The landing of the John T. Brush Stairway. It was built by the New York Giants in 1913 and is the last remaining piece of the Polo Grounds. The stairway will soon be rebuilt with funds provided by all of the major teams (baseball and football Giants, Yankees, Mets, and Jets) that once played there. The inscription on the landing reads as: The John T. Brush Stairway Presented by the New York Giants.

tour and find the *John T. Brush Stairway*. (See *Other Stairs, Other Places* on page 57)

Because I planned to backpack the next day, I cut my time on *The Great Saunter* short by a few miles to save my legs. I ended at the United Nations Building on the east side of Manhattan. So to answer the original question, can you find a crease on the island of Manhattan? The answer is a resounding YES! Creases and opportunities for wandering are everywhere.

Chapter 6

As already mentioned, wandering is not a station-to-station hike and you do have permission to change course. This does not mean that you cannot wander on an established hiking trail or path. A trail is a great place to wander. And if you look around as you walk, you will never cease to wonder at how much there is to see and appreciate – not only nature but also from people who passed through the area before you.

Several years ago I had the opportunity to hike the Appalachian Trail in its entirety from Georgia to Maine.[1] Since then

---

1 In a sense, I came to hiking the Appalachian Trail through wandering. I knew about the Appalachian Trail and had seen it several times, but I had not thought of hiking it end to end. Even though I did plenty of walking, I was not a backpacker at that time. I didn't even own a sleeping bag let alone a backpack or a tent.

That all changed when I read a Civil War diary of one of my wife's relatives through marriage. The diary was written by a soldier who fought for the South as a member of the Army of Tennessee. Near the end of the diary, he describes passing a hot spring in western North Carolina when his unit was marching home after the war. Because my wife and I are both hot springs fans, we decided to check out the spring on an upcoming vacation.

When we visited the hot spring, we discovered that it was only a few hundred feet from the Appalachian Trail. Since we were in the neighborhood, we decided to take a walk on the Trail and liked what we saw. When we got back to town to grab a bite to eat, we noticed that the restaurant had a couple of books about the Trail for sale. We bought one of the books to take home to read.

The timing was perfect; we were considering a major change in our lives and were looking for something special to do in our new life. The Trail fit the bill, and we decided to do an end-to-end hike. It turned out be one of the most profound experiences of my life. Had it not been for the diary, my life could have taken an entirely different direction.

If you are curious about long distance hiking, there are many books you can read including one I wrote in 2002, **Long Distance Hiking on the Appalachian Trail for the Older Adventurer**; New Mountain Books; Albuquerque, NM.

I have returned to the Trail several times to take shorter hikes. Like everyone who goes on a long walk, I took many pictures and have shown them to other people to share the experience. Of all the pictures I took, three stand out the most to me.

The first was of an old apple orchard now gone wild in full blossom right on the trail south of the James River in Virginia. The second was of a New England-style stone wall deep in the woods east of the Hudson River in New York State. And the third was taken from the top of Bear Mountain in Connecticut. That photo shows a landscape of dense trees with perhaps twenty percent of it cultivated.

All three show that before the trail was built the land was used differently than it is today. It is very likely that if you had hiked the Appalachian Trail's route 150 years ago, you would not have gone through wooded mountains; you would have passed small farms, small logging operations and perhaps some mines. And the view from the top of Bear Mountain in Connecticut would have been completely different. The ratio of farmland to woods would have been reversed. The change would have been as radical as that of the waterfront in New York City.

This gave me the idea of revisiting a portion of the Appalachian Trail to take a closer look at prior human impact. Of the three pictures, the one of the old stone wall intrigued me the most, and I decided to examine a portion of the Appalachian Trail east of the Hudson River in New York. My idea was to walk the same distance that a typical long distance hiker would walk in a day (about fifteen or sixteen miles) just to see what someone could discover on the day they hiked through the area.

To develop some context and get some notion of what might be there, I read the trail guides for the area, contacted people responsible for maintaining that section of the trail, and did some research on the Internet. I learned that the area was an important theater of the Revolutionary War and a major iron mining area during the 19th Century.

If you look at a map of the area, the place names on it are begging to be explored. There's Anthony's Nose, Copper Mine Brook, Fort Hill, Little Fort Hill, Fort Defiance Hill, Old West Point Road, Old Albany Post Road, and others. As an aside, if you are having a difficult time coming up with ideas, look at a map. Maps are great places to get ideas for wandering and exploring.

In addition to the place names, I learned there are still the foundations of an old house and barn that were used as a small pox inoculation center during the Revolutionary War right on the trail. I also learned that there was an old mile marker just off the trail on the Old Albany Post Road. In short, there is enough to check out to keep someone wandering for days, months, or perhaps, the rest of one's life in this short span of trail.

But more than anything else I thought it would be interesting to see how many stone walls were still in place from the old abandoned farms along the trail. I knew there were walls, but I didn't remember how extensive they were.

If you were to take this same hike, you would start at the Bear Mountain Bridge in New York State to cross the Hudson River. Very soon after crossing the river you will reach the woods and start making a steep climb to the top. Once you reach the top, you can continue on the Appalachian Trail, or take a side trail to see the bridge you just crossed from high above. If you take the side trail, you will pass two pits that are remnants of a mining operation. This would be a perfect place for a rock hound to look for minerals.

After reaching the viewpoint, which is spectacular, you can then return to the main trail. Immediately upon reaching the trail, you will see the remains of what at one time would have

Looking down at the Hudson River and the Bear Mountain Bridge from the top of Anthony's Nose.

been a well-built road. You could do some exploring and wandering to see where the road goes.

After you walk a few more miles on the Appalachian Trail, you will finally reach your first wall. From there it will be like trying to shut off a blasting fire hose with your bare hands not to see one. Walls are everywhere. They will almost be non-stop. The only place where you won't find one is when you make a steep climb through a rocky hillside. You will find that wherever there is a semblance of a valley or level area, there will be walls. I found that I couldn't keep count, you might do better. I knew that there would be walls, but I had no idea that there would be that many.

The walls are remnants of what once were farms. They provide an amazing wandering opportunity for you. Before checking out the walls, visualize that instead of standing in the middle of a forest, you are standing on cleared land in the middle of a bunch of farms. And that the walls around you are not in the woods but enclosing a working farm field or pasture.

As you walk around and follow the walls, you might be able to find the remains of the farm. You could find an old foundation, a root cellar, a collapsed well, a trash pit, the old garden

Walls were everywhere. Can you imagine what this area must have been like when the farms were still active?

gone wild, or an old orchard; anything that would have shown that this was where people lived and worked. If you take this walk in the fall, you might even be able to pick an apple from the orchard. It could even be an apple that is no longer available at your local produce stand. If you take the walk in the summer, you will definitely have plenty of blueberries. Blueberry bushes are along almost every foot of the trail in this part of the country. As you continue your walk around the old farm, you may want to check out the rockiness of the soil to determine which enclosures were pastures and which ones were used for crops.

And then as you look at the walls, think of all the work that went into building them. After I took this hike, I bought a book on walls[2] and learned that two men with pry bars and an ox with an ox sled could build ten feet of wall in a day. If you look around, you'll see that it must have taken years to build all of these walls. Can you imagine lifting and placing these large rocks on a wall all day long? Can you imagine the size of arms these people must have had and how you would fare if you challenged one of them to an arm wrestling match?

But as you look around, think of how hard their life must have been. When you look at the ground, there are rocks everywhere. Can you imagine trying to support a family on land as unsuitable for farming as this? That's why there are so many trees today. These farms were abandoned as soon as a better opportunity raised its hand.

As you continue up the trail, you will either be going over walls or along them. At one point you may notice an old dirt road no longer usable with walls on both sides of it coming in from the right. The road will make a turn and become the route of the trail. Eventually it will veer off to the left and leave the trail

---

2 *Sermons in Stone: The Stone Walls of New England and New York*; Susan Allport; 1990; W. W. Norton & Company, New York

Where does
this old road
go? The
only way to
find out is
to wander
along it to
see where it
goes.

During the Revolutionary War Little Fort Hill was fortified by Americans to keep British troops from advancing up the Hudson. Today the top of Little Fort Hill is the site of an outdoor chapel just footsteps from the Appalachian Trail.

route. A road like this provides another opportunity for you to wander and explore. Did the road connect the farms to a local community center? If you followed the road far enough would you find remains of an old commercial establishment or a burial ground? Or would it take you to a modern housing development and dump you into someone's backyard? The only way to find out is to wander down the road to see where it will take you.

One of the place names along the trail that caught my attention while I was researching the trail was *Little Fort Hill.* The name, Little Fort Hill, dates back to Revolutionary War and the trail goes right over its shoulder. When you reach the hill, there will be a little side trail weaving through the rocks to get you to the top. Instead of finding remains of a fort, you will find a large statue of Jesus and an outdoor chapel built by the nearby Graymoor Monastery. I found it to be quite a surprise just a few feet off the trail.

Evidence of human occupation will not be the only thing you'll find. There will be the incredible textures of trees growing around rocks, and you might stir up a couple of snakes or other wildlife. When I approached a tiny brook, I disturbed a sunbathing salamander. He immediately jumped into the brook for a quick dip. But rather than swimming away, the salamander kept his nose and eyes out of the water just to see what was going on. I'm not sure who was more curious, me or the salamander. After a few minutes of the two of us watching each other, I moved on.

The Old Albany Post Road dates back to colonial times and is one the oldest unpaved roads still in use in the country. This milemarker is only a few hundred feet from the Appalachian Trail and the hustle and bustle of downtown Manhattan is only 55 miles away.

As you move along you will find more walls and will eventually find the foundations of the Revolutionary War inoculation station. If you detour off the trail for a few minutes at the Old Albany Post Road, you should be able to find the old mile marker. It says that New York City is only 55 miles away.

Just think about it. Everything you have just walked by could easily be covered by a long distance hiker in a day. Can you imagine seeing and experiencing this much every day for several months? And everything on this particular walk just happens to be within commuting distance of the nation's largest city. When I made the walk, I took a bus from New York City to Bear Mountain State Park. When I finished the walk 15 or 16 miles up the trail, a passerby gave me a ride to a commuter train station only a few miles away. Within an hour and ten minutes I was in Grand Central Station in the heart of Manhattan.

And to answer the question, is it possible to wander on an established hiking trail? Again, the answer again is a resounding YES!

Chapter 7

I f you happen to pick up a male-oriented outdoor or health magazine the next time you're waiting at the doctor's office, you would think that everyone venturing outdoors is an Olympic athlete with Hollywood good looks risking his or her life on an extreme adventure. Don't let that discourage you; the outdoors is for everyone. None of the wandering examples in this book require a significant financial outlay or any special athletic ability. Nor do they require a serious time commitment, as all can be done within a day's outing. If you are in decent health and have reasonable stamina, you can probably do every one of these activities. Wandering is an accessible activity.

There is nothing wrong with the extreme activities you read about. Anything that gets you outside and active is good. My concern regarding extreme activities is that some of them can only be done by a very small percentage of the population, and if the extreme is presented as the norm or as the only option, it might create an artificial barrier that could discourage some people from venturing outdoors. This would be unfortunate as there is so much you can do outdoors that is not extreme.

Continuing with this thought, ordinary people are getting out and making significant discoveries all the time. You do not need an advanced degree or a grant from an academic foundation to find something extraordinary. News sources frequently have stories about people like you and me making exceptional finds.

A few years ago, my local newspaper[1] ran a story about a retired geologist finding the remains of a meteor impact crater from many millions of years ago. At the time the article was written, there were only 174 confirmed impact craters in the world. Considering the age of the world, it is not too much of a stretch to say that there are probably more out there for someone to notice.

Any visible trace of the crater in question eroded away a long time ago but the shock patterns from the impact still remains in the rock. The retired geologist discovered the impact crater while hiking with his dog in the mountains near Santa Fe, New Mexico. During the hike he noticed that many of the rocks had an unusual pattern in them. He immediately suspected that they were shock patterns and had his hunch confirmed when he showed sample rocks to other geologists.

In the same vein, there was another article[2] about a man who found the bones of an extinct mammoth eroding out of a creek bank. Creeks can be great places to wander as items of interest are always eroding out creek banks.

I personally am always looking for ideas of possible wandering projects. I sometimes think that the only reason I get the paper, look at various newspapers online, and read magazines is to look for ideas. Ideas for wandering can be found in many places. In the previous chapter I mentioned that maps are a good place for wandering ideas. Just look at one. It is amazing what you can find on a map: intriguing place names, unusual topographic features, old mines, ruins, ghost towns, cemeteries, old

---

1 *Santa Fe Sits on the Site of a Comet or Asteroid Impact, Geologists Say* by John Fleck, ***Albuquerque Journal***, December 17, 2006

2 *Amateur Digger Finds Ancient Bones in Northern N.M.* by Jessica Dyer, ***Albuquerque Journal***, December 27, 2010

Chapter 7

corridors, old Indian treaty lines to name a few. To get an idea of what a topo map can offer, you can check the map examples on pages 66 and 67.

Or, if you are lucky, you might find an annotated historical map for a state, county or neighborhood that is full of ideas. I happened to find one for Socorro County, New Mexico that shows the locations of old cavalry forts, the route the Confederate Army took during the Civil War, old silver mines, cattle drive trails, and Indian raiding routes. Someone could mine that map for a lifetime of places to explore.

When you come across a potential idea, it makes sense to have a method to save that information so you don't forget about it. It could be months or years before you have the opportunity to follow up on that idea. Whatever method you adopt for saving ideas, it should be accessible and useful to you. I personally use a combination of notebooks and file folders to keep track of ideas. Before I go on a business trip or vacation I check my notebooks and folders to see if there is anything I can incorporate into the trip.

In Chapter 5, I mentioned that I made a brief detour while on *The Great Saunter* to check out the John T. Brush Stairway. In this case, I had noticed a little blurb on the Internet some time ago about New York City planning to renovate the last remaining piece of the Polo Grounds. Because I am a long-time baseball fan, this caught my attention and I did some research to learn more about the stairs. This particular item may not make it to your list but there was enough there for me to add it to mine. So when I planned a trip to New York to walk in *The Great Saunter*, I had the information on the John T. Brush Stairway readily available. When I saw how close it was to the route of the *Saunter*, I added it to my agenda. These little add-ons can spice up an adventure to make the overall experience special for you.

Ironically when I was on *The Great Saunter* and made a detour to check out the stairway, a couple of people who were walking with me at the time asked me how I managed to come up with so many different ideas for my trip to New York. As just described, it is quite simple; keep track of your ideas and incorporate them into your planning. In a sense this is really adding the mindset of wandering to your planning. It is really looking at things in a different way in order to **see**.

■ ■ ■

Although this is a hiking- and walking-oriented book, the mindset of wandering can be used in many ways. When added to your planning, it can turn even the most tedious of activities into an exciting journey. I recently had to make a long driving trip during the hottest time of the year to attend a conference. Before I left, I scanned my notebooks to see what I could check out and do along the way. This paid off. Even though I spent most of my time behind the steering wheel, I managed to watch baseball games in three different cities, visit two state highpoints, walk on the last remaining Cahokian Indian Mound inside the city limits of St. Louis, and eat a fried onion cheeseburger (a local specialty) in El Reno, Oklahoma. These and many other things made the trip more than a long hot drive to a conference.

Several years ago my wife and I had the opportunity to take time off from work and spend several months driving around the continent checking things out. On one of our adventures we knew we had to be back in Chicago in three weeks for a doctor's appointment. Our only planned activity was to spend a day with one my sisters in Wisconsin. Other than that the three week time slot was wide open.

While at my sister's, we saw in the newspaper that the National Lumberjack Championships would be held in northern

Wisconsin later in the week. Because my wife had always wanted to see a lumberjack championship we pointed our car towards northern Wisconsin. While there, we figured that since we were so far north that we might as well head east towards Canada to check out a meteor impact crater near Sudbury, Ontario. I had read about the crater several years before and had it on my list as something that I would eventually like to check out.

When we reached Sudbury we realized that we were on a direct line to Ottawa and Montreal, two towns that we had not visited, and we headed in that direction after checking out the crater. We then continued on to the northern part of New York State. While grabbing a bite to eat in Ticonderoga, New York, I saw a newspaper lying on the lunch counter. The lead article was about it being the Baseball Hall of Fame weekend in Cooperstown, New York. The article went on to say that Nellie Fox, my all-time favorite ballplayer, would be inducted the next day. Needless to say we were on our way to Cooperstown.

The entire three week time slot was a case study of employing the mindset of wandering to direct one's life. What we discovered in one place determined where we went next. This led us from one incredible surprise to another. I even managed to shake Muhammad Ali's hand when we bumped into him at the Rock and Roll Hall of Fame in Cleveland. The entire three weeks were amazing.

You can even adapt the mindset of wandering to something as obscure as checking out a grocery store when out of town. Not necessarily going through the aisles to buy supplies, but to notice what is different. Despite the apparent sameness that appears across the country, there are regional and local differences and you can sometimes spot them at a grocery store. What products are featured or prominently stocked to cater to the distinct needs of the local community? What products are not available back home? What would someone from out of town find in your local grocery store? With your developed awareness, you'd be surprised what you see and learn.

For instance, in Navajo country in western New Mexico and eastern Arizona, *fry bread* made of flour and lard and *mutton* are

(Left) In Albuquerque a 20-pound bag of flour is an afterthought and is almost hidden on the bottom shelf. Drive two hours west to Navajo country, it's a completely different story. (Below) There a 20-pound bag of flour is given major prominence. How big is the display for 20-pound bags of flour at your store?

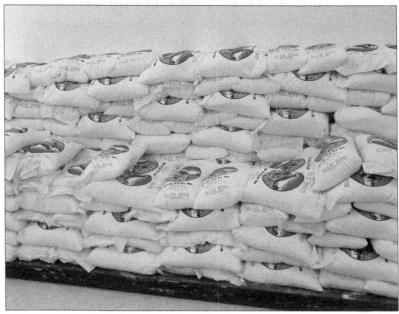

basic staples. If you go to a grocery store in Gallup, New Mexico, the store will have several shelves or bins full of 20-pound bags of flour. The store will also have lard in 25-pound tubs and mutton in the meat department. 130 miles to the east in Albuquerque a 20-pound bag of flour is at best an afterthought and it will only command a small amount of shelf space. Unless you go to a specialty store, you won't find a 25-pound tub of lard or any mutton in Albuquerque. These are the types of differences that you can notice when you wander in a grocery store as you travel across the country.

The mindset of wandering can also help you follow your passions. If you have a passion such as traveling across the country to photograph graveyards, think of what you could do with a project like that? You could tell the story of America and how our conglomeration of differences makes us who we are.

Compare a burial ground in a small Hispanic community in the Southwest to a Puritan graveyard in New England. Could anything be more different? And then compare how both of them are way different than a big city cemetery. I know from having lived in Chicago that certain ethnic groups took meticulous care of the family grave site and had pictures of the deceased etched into the tombstone.

As a bonus, think of all the walking you would get in while wandering amidst the tombstones. And to add to that bonus you could check out other things along the way as you traveled from graveyard to graveyard. This accumulation of activities would transfer your experience from a single mission trip to a wandering adventure.

■ ■ ■

Returning to the topic of obtaining ideas for a wandering adventure, you don't have to read about what someone else did to get an idea. You are free to develop your own ideas. I recently took my dogs for a hike in the Sandia Mountains in New Mexico, not too far from where I live. Instead of taking our usual route, we continued on a lightly used trail. We eventually came upon a large fir tree and my search image capabilities spotted something strange on the tree. It was a silver colored medallion that said *Stamp Act Tree*.

Later on I asked another hiker about the tree. He told me that he saw another tree with a medallion that said *Magna Carta Tree*. I later learned that there is apparently someone who hikes in the Sandia Mountains to look for very large trees. When he finds one, he takes a core sample and counts the rings when he gets home to see how old it is. (Archaeologists do something similar when they take core samples from beams and posts to determine when a structure was built.)

Once he determines the age of the tree, he prepares a medallion and names the tree for an event that occurred in the year the tree germinated. He then returns to the tree and mounts the medallion. The medallion tree that I saw germinated in 1765 when the Stamp Act was passed.

Whoever is doing this is doing it anonymously without official sanction. Regardless, this is an example of someone who has creatively combined his skills and knowledge into his hiking. Is there something similar that you would be interested in doing?

Another example of someone who developed his own adventure is my uncle. He lives north of San Diego and is in his mid-70s. He and a few of his friends came up with the idea of walking the beach near where they live 35 miles or so to downtown San Diego. They have now made this trek several times.

They are not ultra-marathoners doing this in one sitting. In their case, they begin from where they live and start walking along the beach. After they have had enough walking, after about six or seven miles, they walk to the nearest train station or bus stop and take public transportation back home. When they resume the walk a day or two later, they take the train or bus back to where they left off and then continue south along the ocean for another six or seven miles and then take the bus or train back home. They repeat this process until they finally make it to downtown San Diego.

And what a great way to wander; if you can't find something interesting along the beach, you have your eyes closed. There's the surf, seals, seagulls, attractive sunbathers, seashells, driftwood, and whatever else you might find along the shore. And then there are the obstacles you have to navigate around to continue walking along the edge of the continent. There are the mouths of streams to cross, cliffs and rocks to climb over or to detour around, and sand dunes to walk up and over or around. No matter how you cut it, it all adds up to a great trek.

Their adventure illustrates another aspect of wandering. You can wander for as long as you are able to get around. My uncle and his friends are in their mid-70s and they still comb the beach. They do it at their own pace, but they do it.

I know of a man who is now too old to hike in the mountains or to scramble in the backcountry. But every day he walks the alleys near his home, and every day he finds something special. One day it could be a flower blooming; the next day it could be a small animal burrowing under a storage shed; and on the next it could be a small piece of furniture that someone tossed in the garbage that he can take home to repair and refinish. He sees all of this and finds joy in all of this because through his wandering he has connected to the world around him. What would you find of interest if you walked down an alley near your home?

■ ■ ■

If you are still having trouble motivating yourself to wander, consider the discussion at the very beginning of this book regarding context. It may be that you have not found something with a compelling enough context to get you out. There are many people today who were never hikers but now go out *geocaching* or *letterboxing* on regular basis. It may be that they had not found a compelling enough context in a hike per se to get going. But by combining a hike with a handheld GPS device to go on a "treasure hunt", they added that little bit extra to make the context compelling enough to get them started.

Once you are compelled to get going, you too can now start wandering. And once you do that, as shown in this book, you will always find something interesting and never run out of adventures.

■ ■ ■

And this brings us to a final question, what is wandering really all about and why should someone care? Certainly it is fun to go out and see what you can discover and then learn more about what you found. Who doesn't like to find something? And of course it's good for your health to be outside and moving your body. But what wandering is ultimately about is giving you the chance to be right here, right now.

By wandering you can separate yourself, if even for only a brief moment, from your usual routine and actually live in the present. And when you can spend time in the present you can connect to a world that is more than just you. As you do this, you will soon become grateful for being allowed to be part of it. Or as Thomas Merton, the twentieth-century Catholic mystic, said in his book, *New Seeds of Contemplation*:

What is serious to men is often trivial in the sight of God.
What in God might appear to us as "play" is perhaps what He Himself takes most seriously.
At any rate the Lord plays and diverts Himself in the garden of His creation,
and if we could let go of our own obsession with what we think is the meaning of it all,
we might be able to hear His call and follow Him in His mysterious, cosmic dance.

An Invitation

When I started working on this book, I thought that it would be a "how to" on exploring the backcountry. As I progressed I realized that the same skills that I used in exploring and wandering in the backcountry applied to all settings. And that it was the seeing, connecting, and enjoying the world around you no matter where you were that was important. As a result I removed much of the backcountry skill material and concluded the book with Thomas Merton's interpretation of seeing, connecting, and enjoying.

I also need to mention that it was a lot of fun going on the various wandering adventures described in the book and discovering how the skillsets of wandering could be applied in different settings. I hope you too will have as much fun as I did and will discover what is already here for you to enjoy.

I expect to continue wandering and plan to share any special adventures and new insights on a blog at the book's website. The website also includes access to the backcountry skills information that was removed from this book. If you are interested, there is a place on the website for you to share your own wandering ideas and comments. I invite you to visit the book's website at www.gentleartofwandering.com.

Acknowledgements

Although the ideas presented in this book are my own and are a result of what I have absorbed over a long period of time, a book of this nature couldn't have been done without considerable help along the way. First I would like to thank BLM archaeologists, Gretchen and Tony, for their instruction and guidance on the archaeology front. I would also like to thank everyone who shared their stories, accompanied me on hikes and walks, read the manuscript at different stages of its development, and gave me pointers.

Writing may be something you do alone, but it is also something you can't do by yourself. I would never have finished this book without the ideas my archaeology wandering partner, Bob Julyan, and my wife Claudia provided.

I would also like to thank Anne Stehr and my sister Carolyn Ryan for their art and design work in giving this book its look and feel.

Finally I would like to mention *Pilgrim at Tinker Creek* by Annie Dillard. Page 81, of her book references the 1927 book *The Gentle Art of Tramping* by Stephen Graham. I managed to find a copy of the Graham book and read it. Although it speaks to a different time and place, its underlying message of getting out, connecting to the moment, and enjoying all that the outdoors has to offer still rings true. I hope my adaptation of the title does the same.

Contact Information:

Contact the Author
David Ryan
612-889-9640
davidryan@msn.com
www.gentleartofwandering.com
www.newmountainbooks.com

Ordering Information:

Call: 612-889-9640
E-mail: davidryan@msn.com
Write:
New Mountain Books
2324 Rio Grande Boulevard NW
Albuquerque, NM 87104
www.newmountainbooks.com

The Gentle Art
of
Wandering